Señor Lard Arse & Fat Man

A journey around the Iberian coastline of Spain & Portugal

Martin Barber

Contents

Acknowledgements

I could be here all day endlessly saying thank you for helping this book and journey to become a reality. The first really big thank you has to be to Vanessa, my wife, for always encouraging me to follow my dreams. She really is a true inspiration and my best friend in the world.

Dave was great throughout the whole journey round the Iberian coastline, from our drunken state of hatching the idea to helping me get through the bike test and ride the route. He's forever a very good friend and it's a real pleasure to have been on the journey with him. I just hope I didn't slow you down too much Dave.

I have to thank Caroline, Dave's wife, as not only did he miss their wedding anniversary because he was with me fishing and getting drunk when we hatched the idea of this trip in Spain, but he also missed it the following year too because we were somewhere in the Pyrenees again, probably trying to get drunk but having a whale of a time whilst on this great adventure.

I could give a whole list now but it's much easier to just say thank you to IRT (Ipswich Rider Training), Graham and Shirley, for getting me through the motorcycle test at my first attempt. It was not easy, especially when I either missed or failed the theory.

And thank you to MotoMercado motorcycle hire shop in Marbella, and Jac for a great bike and service for the whole bike hire period, as well as turning a blind eye to the slight damage caused by my small accident on the second day of the journey.

A huge thank you to Ivan my editor for his tireless work deciphering the drivel I originally wrote and for turning it into a read that now makes sense. I hope that in the future he will be just as eager to take on such a project, knowing just what state the book would reach him in. Only time will tell.

Not forgetting everyone else who helped me and Dave with this journey and the book that came with it.

Introduction

It was a bright early September morning in 2017, just around the corner from St Pauls in central London, when I left the building. I knew that was my last day in the job. I had planned to just pop in, say a few goodbyes and clear my bits from the desk prior to taking a coffee just around the corner with a good family friend. I can't say I was sad to be leaving after thirty-five years in the construction industry; I was well worn out and in need of a new challenge.

I had been reading several books, including about cycling around the world, the best of which I thought was *World Cycling Stripped Bare* by Sean Conway – his memoirs of his journey around the world, all the good and bad times on the way. It all sounded just up my street – a little bit of man-alone time fighting the road and sleeping wherever I dropped – but not at my age, and I hadn't been on a bicycle for over thirty years. Around the world? I doubt I could make it around the village!

I read some great adventures of expeditions on motorcycles too, travelling throughout the world, from mountains high to jungles, and unseen animals through the worlds of lost civilisations. My favourite of these books was *Ride to the Midnight Sun*, written by motorcycle enthusiast, Stephen Mason – what a read. Having read this adventure of his travels to the northernmost point in Norway and back from his home town in Scotland, he made it all sound so much fun, as well as something we could all achieve with a little effort.

I was sure there was something out there for me but what it was I had no idea. My problems were that I wasn't so young anymore and how could I fund such an adventure? These were questions I was to answer very soon indeed. But I had a seed solidly planted. My time would come – I didn't know what, where or how – but it was there, knocking on my door every spare minute of my day.

The coming weeks and months would provide a potential solution. We (that is my wife Vanessa and I) were planning to visit my son and his family in southern Spain. My good friend Dave, who has over the years come to be known as 'Fat Man', and who refers to me as 'Mr Lard Arse', along with his lovely wife Caroline, would be visiting us out in Spain for a few days. Dave had planned to stay on for a short while on his own once

Caroline had returned, as she had work commitments. So we could hopefully get a few days of sea fishing in together and share a few Spanish beers.

I was really looking forward to spending quality time with Vanessa after a very long and stressful final works contract. She too had not had the best of years, with several small operations to assist the onset of osteoarthritis in her left foot. She needed this time to recuperate in Spain, enjoying the warm sun-drenched days and even warmer evenings. Together, we both looked forward to this and the time with our family in the Spanish sunshine.

For me, I did have this nagging little gremlin banging away inside my mind, telling me that all I needed now was a direction to focus on after finishing work and going into a self-enforced semi-retirement. What could that be? Could I find my own adventure to focus on without breaking the bank? Would it give me a focus for the year ahead, as well as being fit enough in my early fifties to actually enjoy the experience?

Chapter 1

How the Journey Began

Whoever tells you that after thirty-five years of being self-employed, when you decide to stop work it ends right away – how wrong they are! I was in southern Spain, Fuengirola to be exact, seven kilometres of sandy beaches, and a never-ending supply of restaurants and cuisine from all over the world, all selling their wares to the never-ending supply of holidaymakers who arrive daily on the shores. We had rented a beach apartment for six weeks, with two bedrooms so friends and family could visit us as we tried to chill and relax. I had brought out my beach casting rods and was looking forward to feeding the fish on the beach, as I always seem to do, and falling asleep in the sun. Paradise, if I say so myself.

The problem is, I was still getting emails and phone calls for help and advice from my old employers. Not the best start to my early retirement, I can tell you. Hopefully, I thought to myself, they will get the message if I just turn the phone off for a few days, which is just how I dealt with the situation.

One week into our Spanish adventure and we were enjoying endless time with our granddaughter, who was growing up so fast. Our son and his wife were making time to ensure we got to see them as much as possible. This was such a great treat for us, as all three of our sons have travelled incessantly over the past ten years and we have not had too much time together with any or all of them. So when such times arrive you really do have to make the best of them.

Turning the phone back on it appeared that work had finally got the message to leave me alone. They had called only a few times and sent no emails for two days either, so fingers crossed their world wouldn't fall apart now I had gone. On the other hand, my friend Dave had messaged and asked if all was okay for their coming visit. In fact, he had messaged again and again to ask if we were okay, as he could not get hold of us. With my phone turned off I had forgotten that Dave would not be able to message me, although he could have messaged Vanessa, but then that would mean using the grey matter he had inside the wind tunnel directly between his ears, which was never going to happen.

I messaged Dave just to let him know I was alive and to apologise for my phone being out of order for the past few days. We discussed his and Caroline's arrival and what we could do when the two of them arrived. Close by is the lovely small village of Mijas Pueblo, and the tapas bars are absolutely amazing. Dave, like me, thinks with his stomach, but then I'm of the opinion that most men my age do too. So that was the first day planned. Caroline was staying only for the weekend as she had work to return to on the coming Monday.

They arrived on the Thursday, and late in the evening we all headed back to the apartment to enjoy a cold beer and glass of wine, whilst looking out over the Spanish Costa del Sol. With the warmth of the late summer evenings it was just lovely.

We headed up into Mijas Pueblo the following day and just enjoyed a lazy day mooching around this beautiful village. Its whitewashed houses line the tightly packed streets that are so narrow that it's a wonder that cars can drive though. Colourful plant pots hung from the walls throughout the village – it really is a picture-perfect Spanish village. Then it was off for the tapas lunch as discussed; small helpings of traditional Spanish dishes of bite-sized fish and meat cuisine, wonderful sauces, and with a cold beer to wash it all down.

We enjoyed the weekend, walking along the beach, round the port in Fuengirola. We also took an afternoon out on the Sunday to Puerto de la Duquesa, a lovely small fishing harbour to the west of Fuengirola, about an hour away, great for just walking along the never-ending promenade, taking a glass of wine or beer and just enjoying your time out. It really was such a shame Caroline had to return that evening, but I assured her I would look after Dave in her absence. She in return looked hard at me and assured me she knew we would both end up in trouble together. How right she can be sometimes.

Having arrived back at the apartment after delivering Caroline to the airport in Malaga on time for her flight back to the UK, we all shared a beer and just relaxed in the heat of the Spanish evening. Vanessa was struggling to walk too far as her foot was still hurting after her latest small operation, so Dave and I decided we would walk down to the port of Fuengirola the next day to check out the fishing boats and find a skipper for the Tuesday.

It was another warm morning on the Monday, so we walked into the port area, about an hour away from the apartment, and headed into the information office. A nice lady behind the desk spoke great English and she found us a local skipper who would be setting sail at 9am on the Tuesday for the day and at a great price of €50. A bargain, if I say so myself, especially as beer and soft drinks were also included. We then took a brief walk around the port area, looking for opening times of the local restaurants and cafés just to make sure we could grab breakfast the following day prior to boarding our fishing trip. Then it was a brisk walk back to meet Vanessa for a sandwich and cold beer for lunch and to relax on the beach for the day.

On Tuesday, Dave and I walked down to the port early to grab breakfast at under €6 for a full English. We could not complain at the price or the plate full of food offered for the price. We washed it down with the house special of the morning, a coffee and brandy. At €1.80 for a large black coffee with what seemed like a triple brandy with it, I did suggest to Dave that we should maybe stay and drink coffee all day just for the hell of it. He did point out that the beer on the boat was free and came with what we hoped would be a bag full of fish too. I really could not argue with that, so we polished off the brandy and made our way to the boat.

Our skipper was a local man. His English was not the best but he did manage to collect the outstanding balance of our fee very well, as we questioned whether we were actually on the right boat. There were several other people waiting to board for the day's sport too.

Out we set for the fishing. Dave and I were out on the front of the boat with two guys from South Africa, and they were a great sport, having a very similar sense of humour to me and Dave too. At the rear of the boat were approximately six or seven people, including a family with a small boy of around ten years of age, so being out at the front seemed a good place to be.

As we headed out, the swell began to get deeper by the minute, and before too long we were ten feet higher or lower than when we started, but through all this the guys from South Africa braved the journey back to the skipper's room for more beer. Fishing started well and I managed to bag two small sea bream before my luck ran out for the day. I should say that for the brief period of thirty minutes that I had caught and Dave had not, I did remind him once or twice that we were here to catch fish! Mind you, within an hour Dave was the one instructing me on what I should and should not be doing with the rod in my hand … in more ways than one.

After about three hours it was clear that the swell was not going to improve. It was at this time that the beer also seemed to be calling. At least with my backside nailed to the deck I could not fall over, and even the South Africans had the same idea, although Dave carried on with his one-man fishing trip, to make sure there were no late winners in the competition. He hauled in double figures for the day, although they were, if I recall, all smaller than my two!

The sea didn't improve and we headed back after a head count from the skipper, and a vote from everyone on who wanted to stay out fishing in this rollercoaster boat, or who wanted to go back to port. It was 11-0 in favour of dry flat land, so the skipper turned us around and off we headed back to port.

Landing back in port it was no surprise that we both headed straight into the first bar/restaurant by the boat. The temperature was in the high twenties, with clear blue skies, but most importantly the ground was not moving. Beers were soon on the table and we were enjoying our day out.

Vanessa had messaged whilst we were out to let me know she would be out for the day and evening, babysitting our granddaughter. We were on our own for the day and had to fend for ourselves; no mean feat, I can tell you. It was like the blind leading the blind now. If I said we stopped at a few bars on what should have been a one-hour walk back, which was to take us seven hours in total, it's probably a good summary of the afternoon.

We chatted about my latest job completion and the fact that Dave had been retired for over two years now, and how he was enjoying it. He had been out to Mexico earlier in the year with friends on a motorcycle tour and the whole ethos of the trip and his adventure was great to listen to for me.

It was in an Indian restaurant just before we finally got back that we again got on to the subject of the bike trip he had been on previously, and Dave said his next big dream would be to ride the whole of the Iberian coastline. Spain and Portugal by coast – now that sounds like an adventure. Mind you, I did jokingly say to Dave that I would come too but we would have to do it on 125cc bikes, as I don't have a bike licence. Dave quickly jumped at the idea and between the three of us – yes that's Dave, me and the beer talking – we had sort of hatched some kind of plan to travel around the coast of Spain and Portugal on two 125cc bikes.

Well, the next thing I can remember from that night was waking up the next morning to Vanessa having a few short stern words about how she'd had to get Dave out of bed, as she had rung the bell several times when she arrived home but I was fast asleep in the land of nod. Dave also thought it great fun to keep reminding me all day about the fact I had abandoned Vanessa for the night whilst I slept and he had been like a knight in shining armour, coming to the rescue of my damsel in distress.

We had a lazy day on the Wednesday. In truth we both had a sore head, so it was nice to just chill and recharge after the day before. By late afternoon Vanessa was feeling up to a walk so we headed down to the promenade along the Fuengirola beach line. We stopped for a small beer in a couple of places, each time reminding ourselves or asking the question of whether we had or had not been in this place the day before. Vanessa took great sport in winding us both up about the whole affair, and in fairness she was entitled to.

It was on our way back that we noticed a huge motorcycle hire shop just off the seafront. Dave insisted we should go in and see just what we could hire for our bike trip and to get an idea of cost. When we looked at what was on offer, the best option seemed to be the twist and go Yamaha scooters. The shop assistant assured us that even with me and Dave on them, they would hold a good speed of 120–130kph. It was a basic plan and we were now looking at 125cc Yamaha scooters for the trip. I discussed details with the shop assistant and took their email address so I could contact them regarding price etc. for the two scooters, and the time period and distance we would require for the rental period. They could not have been more helpful, and Dave and I left the shop with quite a buzz that day, with a feeling that something was about to happen. All we had to do now was agree on exactly where we wanted to go, the route for the trip, work out an approximate kilometre total, and estimate how long it would take us.

We had lunch on the way back to the apartment that day in one of the beach restaurants, and Vanessa ordered her favourite barbecued sardines, cooked in one of the Spanish fishing boats set up as a barbeque. I was still a little delicate and settled for just a plate of chips, whilst Dave, true to form, tucked into a whole sea bream cooked in sea salt.

An hour or two later we were back on the balcony watching the world go by again, sipping on a cold beer, planning the route we might take and using Google Maps to get an approximate kilometre range of the journey. It was looking like 4,000–4,500km (about 2,500–2,750 miles). The only real agreement on the route was that we should start and finish in the Fuengirola area of Spain, as that is where we would be the following summer, once again enjoying our granddaughter and family time.

So the basic plan had been hatched. No time or date had been agreed but we were looking at starting in twelve months' time – so September 2018 (ish) it was. We were both excited about the prospect of the trip, and Dave said he would have to discuss it with Caroline on his return home, which was absolutely no problem. Caroline, however, jumped at the idea. She thought it would be great for the two of us to have some male bonding time. I think secretly she was just over the moon to get rid of him for the three weeks!

Espańia here we come – it's Señor Lard Arse and Fat Man on the Iberian tour 2018 ...

Chapter 2

From a 125cc Scooter to a Real Bike

After Dave's return to the UK, Vanessa and I enjoyed the rest of our time out in Spain with the family. Vanessa's mum and dad even visited for a long weekend and we celebrated our granddaughter's first birthday too. However, it wasn't long before it was time to leave and head back to reality.

Dave and I kept in touch but didn't really mention the trip much for a month or two. It wasn't until early December at a Christmas meal and disco night in a local hotel close to where Dave lives, when we were enjoying a night out with Dave and Caroline and one or two other friends, that the trip came up again. Once again both Dave and I had had one too many beers (this is becoming quite a regular thing now!) and we started telling the rest of the table just what we were signing up to, as though it was planned right down to the last detail.

You really can't beat the sound of 80s music and a few beers inside you to get the old grooves going on the dance floor. But try as we all did, we could not get Dave up for a boogie. Caroline and Vanessa were really enjoying themselves and I kept being dragged back to the dance floor for another groove before sneaking back for a top-up and a chat with Dave. It's surprising just how brave or stupid you can be when full of beer.

It was later in the evening that Caroline mentioned it would be so much more fun on a real bike when we went on our bike trip and not one of those girly scooters we were looking at using. Thinking back, I'm starting to wonder just how much Caroline had drunk that night too, or was she in cahoots with Dave in what was about to happen?

You need to know that Caroline is also a competent biker in her own right. If I remember right, that's how Dave originally wooed her and how they got together; something along the lines of 'would you like a ride on my big one' is how Dave tells the story! Caroline, on the other hand, relates the story somewhat differently, and seems to recall she thought she was taking pity on him as he was close to retirement age and in need of company that particular day. I might be wrong, but I tend to believe Caroline's version of events. Who am I to argue with a woman?

So there we are, dancing away and enjoying the festive mood, when with a somewhat beer-induced confidence, I quickly stated that I agreed with Caroline regarding the bike. I looked straight at Dave and told him he should use his bike, and that it was crazy him hiring a scooter when he had the means to travel anyway, especially as he actually had three bikes: a BMW K1300S, a BMW S1000R and an Aprilia RSV 1000R. So, the thought of him hiring a bike did seem quite ludicrous when he could quite simply start his own hire shop with the number of bikes he had floating about.

I was feeling very confident now, and with the beer fuelling my ever-opening mouth, informed everyone it would be easy for me to just book up to take a crash course in motorcycling, take my test and join Dave on a real bike, not just the scooters we had planned originally. Yes, you can see the kind of hole I was digging myself into. Dave agreed it was a great idea, although I'm sure he knew it would not be as easy as I thought it would be in the inebriated state I was in that night. I'm sure he was laughing inside at the challenge I had just set myself and had informed most of my close friends of.

I woke the following morning in Dave's spare room. I must have been on the bitter the night before as there was a familiar smell in the air. I can assure you it wasn't roses! I made my way downstairs to the kitchen to put the kettle on and left Vanessa sleeping in the bed. Dave appeared within five minutes and the first thing he complained about was the smell of sewerage upstairs, and asked whether I had smelled it. I didn't have the heart to tell him I was the culprit and just said I hadn't noticed it when I got up …

Dave made some toast and I finished the brew, then we started discussing the night before and my new direction for the bike trip. Dave had a few suggestions, as several years ago he had also taken a crash course for his motorcycle licence and he recommended a local company in Ipswich. I made a note of their name and told him I would look them up later when I was feeling more alive.

A day or two later Vanessa and I were sorting out our diary, as during the winter months we have been running our Austrian ski chalet business for the past eight years. It's a small hobby business we run in a house we bought back in the mid-2000s and renovated ourselves. We don't make money from the business, but what we do make ensures we can run the house throughout the year and be there through the winter to enjoy the great winter sports that we have on our doorstep. The added bonus is we get to meet so many like-minded people who rent out apartments and share the beautiful area we have been visiting for many years. You would be surprised at just how many friends you have when you own a ski property and they all want a free holiday.

With the winter commitments in hand, this meant I would not be able to look at taking my test until at least May, and that was providing I could get my theory test completed prior to then too. I called the company in Ipswich (Ipswich Rider Training) and discussed the options for my test with the owner Graham. It's surprising just how different it is when you're fifty-something, setting out to take a test such as a bike test. It bears no resemblance to thirty-five years before when I was taking my car licence. Then everything seemed stressful, and if I failed back then the feeling was more like the end of the world. It's strange how age does that to you; if only it made you sensible too.

Graham was a great guy. I knew straight away I was in the right place, as he explained everything to me, how it could work and that time was no problem. All he asked was that I kept in touch and ensured he had four weeks' notice to fit me in when I needed my schedule of theory, bike test, bike ride. That simple!

So my plan was to use the time during the winter to revise the Highway Code once again after thirty-five years. I would then complete my theory test during mid- to the end of April, maybe the start of May. That would give Graham at Ipswich Rider Training (IRT) four weeks' notice to see what was available for the week's tuition, which would include all of the following as he set out:

Day 1: 9am–4pm full day. CBT (compulsory basic training) on geared 125cc. Confidence building. Start on 125cc and aim to upgrade to 500cc or 650cc by end of day.

Day 2: 9am–4pm full day. Full upgrade followed by focus on Mod1 training for first test – bike control, figure 8, U-turns, emergency stop, swerve, etc.

Day 3: 9am–4pm full day. If Day 2 goes well, we will focus on Mod2 training – road riding, cover all junction types, road types, national speed limit, etc.

Day 4: Escort to test centre for Mod1 test.

Providing Day 3 goes well, we need one days break before Day 5. We can, if needed, fit in some additional riding training if you need it.

Day 5: Escort to test centre for Mod2 test.

Like I said earlier, simple, providing I got the theory out of the way too, prior to starting on the bike.

Chapter 3

Licence to Ride

The plan was laid for me to take my licence and be able to join Dave on the coastal navigation ride of Spain and Portugal, although where most people would be discussing routes and what they wanted to see from the trip, all I could think of was getting the licence. I had even been shopping on my last day in the UK prior to leaving for Austria. I went out with Dave to buy myself a helmet, gloves and boots, which was not cheap either, and here I was buying all the gear and did not even have a bike. Dave also handed down his current summer riding jacket and leggings, complete with linings and waterproofs. He had been to the NEC motorcycle show recently and bought a new outfit for himself, so he handed down the old gear to me, for which I was extremely grateful.

So what I planned to do was buy a thirty-day online training course from the DVLA at the start of March, so I would then have thirty days of revising every day for one or two hours.

That's up to sixty hours' revision, then I'd get my theory test booked for the start of April – that was the plan anyway.

That all changed in early January though, when I was chatting to my good friend Trevor about taking a catfishing holiday in Spain, possibly late April or early May. I couldn't resist the opportunity as I, like my friend Trevor, absolutely love catfishing. The lure of the river Ebro in northern Spain really is a fisherman's dream river; endless carp fishing and catfishing to dream of. So with a fishing holiday to fit in between the theory and the practical bike tests, I had to rearrange so that I would buy the theory course by the third week of March, then I would fly back to the UK in the third week of April to sit the theory before flying out to Spain for the fishing with Trevor. Oh yes, and Dave and my father-in-law, who's known as Jock, would also be coming fishing too now. Life does tend to get complicated sometimes.

So at the end of March I purchased the theory practice and started the online work. My first job was to read the current motorcycle highway book to ensure I was not blind to what was happening. Within a week I had finished the book and moved on to what I thought would be a quite easy online test module. How wrong was I? I took an initial test first to see how I would fare, and at 54% I really did feel embarrassed at how little I knew, especially after thirty-five years of driving. Yes, I do realise riding a motorcycle is not the same as a car, but to be honest, I only realised that after those first few mock tests.

Two weeks into my revision it was the end of our ski season. We were due to drive straight to Spain once again, where we had purchased a nice holiday lodge close to our son and intended to enjoy another great summer with him and his family close by. Furthermore, his twin brother had now moved to live close to him in Spain, so we had the added bonus of both our youngest two sons now living and working together, and they would be close by all year.

What I had not really allowed for was the four-day drive and no revision whilst we travelled from Austria to Spain. Also, when we arrived we would have no internet, so the second two weeks of revision were going to be difficult at best. We arrived in Spain on 9 April, settled into the new lodge and managed to sort out short-term internet access locally. The reception was not great and quite intermittent too, but I did the best I could.

I had managed to book my theory test for 25 April, so I would fly to the UK two days prior, have one final day of revision and then take the test. Two days later, on 27 April, the four of us were flying from the UK to Spain for the fishing holiday. Once I had passed the theory, I was to inform Graham

I had done so, and we could then arrange the test and practice week for the month following. It was that simple.

I crammed as much as I could in on the Tuesday prior to my theory test on the Wednesday. If I'm honest, I was really nervous, and that really is not me. I'm normally the most confident person you know. I took the test and actually thought it went much better than I had imagined. I was back out of the test centre within forty minutes and Dave was waiting to pick me up.

It wasn't until I sat in the car and opened the test certificate that I actually realised I had failed the test by one point. I needed to score 44 out of 50 questions correctly for a pass, but I had scored 43. I was gutted; not only had I arranged a grand tour of Europe to be able to take the theory test but I had gloriously failed it as well. We got back to Dave's house and I tried to rebook a test for the following morning, as we weren't flying until late afternoon. The problem as I found out a little later was that I had to wait seventy-two hours to be able to book a retest.

So, as gutted as I was, it was fishing next. I would have to sort out what I could do to get the theory done but first I needed to discuss that with Vanessa. We spoke, and together agreed it would be cheaper to fly back straight away with everyone after the fishing and do the test, then fly back to the Spain to join her. So I went online and booked my new test for the day after we were due to arrive back from the fishing, and booked a new flight back to the UK with the guys. Fishing was great, but we could not fish for catfish as the Ebro was in full flood. It was disappointing, but the carp fishing we had that week was fantastic and it was good to be away with Trevor, Dave and Jock too.

It was on the first night that Jock suffered a worrying medical problem and I needed to get him to the local hospital at 3am. Our host at the fishing lodge, Paul, was fantastic; he put Jock and me in the car and thirty minutes later we were at the local hospital. Twenty-five minutes after that, Jock had been seen by a specialist and his treatment was in hand, albeit a temporary solution until he returned to the UK. If you do ever read this book Paul, thank you once again from Jock and me for that night.

Jock's medical problem meant that I needed to take him to the hospital on our arrival back in the UK on the very same afternoon. He could then be seen by a specialist in A&E and get the treatment he needed. The next problem was that he needed to be at his doctor's the following day. I called his doctor's first thing in the morning when they opened but there was only an emergency appointment for that day and I had to take him at 2.15pm to see his doctor. He was not able to drive due to his condition, so I would need to take him.

My rearranged theory test was booked that same day for 2.45pm, but that was forty minutes in the wrong direction away from Jock's doctor's. So there was no choice really but to miss the theory test and ensure Jock got the medical advice and medication he needed. I would have to return that evening to Spain as planned and think again, with Vanessa, about how the theory test was going to happen. The important thing for both Vanessa and me was that Jock was fine and in good hands; the test would just have to wait.

It was nice to be back in Spain and to feel the warmth of the sunshine after four months of snow and ice in Austria. Also, with the following month of travelling around Europe for theory tests, holidays and then back to the UK with Jock, I was knackered. I needed a couple of days just to catch up, especially on sleep.

Graham had emailed whilst I was fishing and wanted to know how I was and the information on my theory test. He needed to know whether I was now in a position to get the test and practical booked. He was more worried that if I did not book for the first week of June, he would not now be able to fit me in after that until August, and that was too close to call if it all went wrong. Let's face it, I was starting to feel like my middle name was 'unlucky', with the amount of bad luck I was having now.

I discussed the situation with Vanessa and we arranged for me to fly back to the UK early the following week, arriving at Stansted airport, and from there book the closest theory test centre to the airport that had a free test available at the right time. That was at Harlow, twenty-five minutes by train from the airport. So I flew into Stansted, arriving at 1pm, took the train to Harlow, then walked the 150yds to the test centre from the train station. I was two hours early, but I explained the whole situation to the receptionist and it was my lucky day, they could fit me in in ten minutes for the retest. Pass or fail, I was finally having some luck.

I filled out the paperwork as required, stored all my belongings in my locker and was shown to my test monitor. It must have been because it all happened so fast that I had no nerves. I sat down, took the test and then had twenty minutes checking every answer again and again prior to finishing and walking out. I was given my locker key to collect my belongings and then collected my test results – I had 98%.

Forty-nine correct answers and one wrong. Bingo, I was finally moving to the next stage.

I left the test centre, walked back to the train station and took the next available train back to Stansted airport. I did have four hours to kill before my flight back to Spain that evening, but it was worth it though. Finally I was beginning to feel that luck was on my side.

Having arrived safe and sound and had a good night's sleep it was great to have the monkey off my back regarding the theory test. I called Graham at IRT and he too was pleased. We discussed availability and it was agreed that the best days and test availabilities he could offer would be for me to start on Saturday, 2 June, then take Sunday off, which Graham said I would need after thirty-five years out of the saddle, as I would be stressed and tired after my first day's riding.

I would then move on to two days' full-on training for the Mod 1 practical. He had availability already for 11.30am on the Wednesday, so I could have a further half-day's tuition prior to the test. Providing that went well, I would need to have a twenty-four-hour break prior to the Mod 2 practical test, so that would be on the Friday.

I booked the dates with him there and then and set about looking for flights etc. to suit getting to and from the UK once again. Two hours later and we were all booked up. Both Vanessa and I would come back to the UK for ten days, and we would also be able to see our two grandsons, Callum and Jack, as well as share our eldest grandson, Callum's, birthday party while we were there. Vanessa was also keen to see Jock, her father, after his recent medical problems, so we were all quite jovial at the prospect of getting back for several reasons.

******

Day one of the training week if you remember was:

9am–4pm full day. CBT (compulsory basic training) on geared 125cc. Confidence building. Start on 125cc and aim to upgrade to 500cc or 650cc by end of day.

Vanessa dropped me off in Ipswich, as she did each day that week. I was early, as I always am when it comes to appointments. I met Graham for the first time in the flesh. He was opening up prior to all the students arriving. Several other instructors arrived and they moved off into a back office whilst I awaited notice of what was happening today. I was introduced to Shirley, a local girl, who would be my instructor for the week. She was a lovely lady, in her mid-forties, and had one of those soft Suffolk accents that just put your mind at ease straight away. She also had a great sense of humour and I could see straight away that we were going to get on just fine.

After the obligatory paperwork signing, health and safety talk, and bike awareness talk from Shirley, I was kitted out with my hi-vis gear, plus an intercom system so she could instruct me whilst we were riding. I was shown to a Kawasaki 125cc bike, which would be my baby for the day. This was my only nervous point of the day, as it had been thirty-five years since I had done what I was about to do, ride a bike.

I mounted the bike, remembering to mount from the left, covered the front brake, made sure I pulled in the clutch and pressed the start button – see, all that theory practice was working already. Shirley had already explained that we would be driving in the van a short distance to the IRT off-road area to get me used to the bike and to train me for the CBT test that was coming, hopefully later that day.

Getting serious now, I had a small debrief on how it felt after not having ridden for so long. Shirley did say I looked quite confident and it was obvious I had ridden before. When she asked if I had any questions so far I asked her, "Do I look like a circus clown on this dinky toy bike?"

True to form, Shirley's answer was, "I couldn't have put it better myself." I could see we were friends straight away and that I had a great trainer to get me through this week's rider training.

The day went very quickly, with a lot of figures of eight, roundabout scenarios, road junction practice as well as just going up and down the gears, before we set off for some real on-the-road training. I was starting to realise this was really going to be a great adventure with a bike.

By mid-afternoon I had been upgraded to a man's bike, leaving the Kawasaki behind for a Suzuki SV 650cc. All too soon the first day was over and I must admit my backside was numb. My hands were also quite numb and full of pins and needles too. It turns out that even though I had bought the 3XL gloves, they were slightly too small and were restricting my grip and feel for the brakes and clutch. Shirley sorted out a set of lightweight gloves from the stores for me to carry on with the next day. She couldn't believe they had a set of 4XL gloves in the stores box, and was even more surprised that they had never been opened and still had the plastic binding connecting them together. She laughed and told me I had the biggest hands she had seen.

Vanessa picked me up at 4pm and Shirley had a quick word with her just to inform her I had been a good boy and behaved myself all day. We said goodbye, and I was looking forward to my day off on the Sunday. Graham was right when he said I would be tired and sore after my first day. I slept like a baby that night, and the following morning my backside was still numb.

Day 2 arrived, and today I was looking forward to riding a bike and being promoted from circus clown to learner rider:

9am–4pm full day. Confidence building – start on 125cc and aim to upgrade to 500cc or 650cc by end of day.

I must have impressed on the first day (well that's what I think anyway) as Shirley had the Suzuki 650cc sat outside ready again and prepared for me to carry on my training first thing that morning.

Yippee! I would not be taking out the clown's bike again, thank god. I can't express just how you feel at 6ft 2in, tipping the scales on the wrong side of 16st and having to ride a bike that was built for a seventeen-year-old teenager. At least this bike would not look like I had outgrown it.

It was 9am and we were heading into the tail end of the rush hour traffic in Ipswich. I would be lying if I said I wasn't a little concerned after only one day's training under my belt. Shirley, however, was great, with her constant clear instructions on my road position and time management prior to junctions. So, during all this I was starting to feel confident.

The couple of things I was struggling with were indicators and pulling out of T-junctions. Turning the indicators on was no problem, but with thirty-five years of driving cars and having the indicators automatically turn themselves off after turning right or left, I was getting lazy and forgetting to turn them off. Mind you, I did tell Shirley the only reason I was doing it was to give her something to keep nagging at me for. You can imagine this was just like giving her more ammunition to keep abusing me verbally. There were a few occasions when I lifted my left hand and made the birdy sign – blah, blah, blah – informing her she was abusing me over the intercom. It was a good job all I could do was listen, as I had no mouthpiece, as I might have pushed the boundaries too hard on occasion otherwise.

Pulling away from T-junctions was the other problem. I was either just missing the curb when turning right or was way too close to the centre of the road when turning left. Shirley left me to it for the first two or three junctions before she instructed me to stop looking directly at the road in front of the bike, and to look twenty-five to thirty yards ahead to where I wanted to be when coming out of the junction. She was right. When at the junction, I was ensuring the traffic was good left and right then, as I pulled away, I was looking directly at the road three or four yards ahead. Once I took Shirley's advice of looking further ahead, and let my body automatically steer the bike whilst I was doing this, it was like magic. That might sound simple to most bike riders, but remember I was on my second day's tuition and it felt like I had learned something new, and it was a great feeling to get it right.

We rode through Ipswich, and by 10.30am the traffic was getting better. We took the outside ring road several times and then went into several housing estates to practice the right and left junctions again and again. Before too long it was coming up to 12.30pm and Shirley suggested we head for one of the local supermarkets for a sandwich and a drink. The sun had been out all day and it was nice and warm, about 24°C, and I was feeling a little dehydrated too, so lunch and a drink sounded like a great idea. There was a huge improvement on my backside today though. The bike was bigger and the seat was too, so I was feeling much more comfortable.

After lunch we headed back to the off-road area for another hour's practice on the standing starts and emergency stop. I must admit I was a little wary about building up speed then using the front brake to stop as an emergency. I just had the feeling I could end up over the front wheel. It might just have been me but I was struggling to get to 30mph plus, before hitting the braking area. This feeling was probably down to being on the bike, but I did get there in the end.

Finally I had the U-turn to practice, again using the look ahead, not in front of you, tactics that Shirley had instructed me on for the T-junctions, which worked absolutely fine here too. I was nailing the U-turn every time.

Time was getting on now, so we left the off-road training area and had a trip around the ring road again, heading out towards Felixstowe, where we then joined the A14 and were heading back in the Ipswich/Bury St Edmunds direction. I knew what was coming next, as Shirley started to direct me on to the slip road. I was about to ride over the Orwell Bridge, no mean feat in a car, as it's always very windy, so I did have a little apprehension, being on a bike. The wind was not too bad for my first trip over the bridge. I kept the speed at about 50–55mph and held on for what seemed like a lifetime, but it was over quickly enough and Shirley was happy too.

Coming off at the A12 junction, we then headed back on the road into Ipswich and to the IRT offices. Another day over and I was really enjoying the training, and I was another day closer to the bike licence. I felt much better today; not as tired as the Saturday, as I had enjoyed almost all of the day, and my backside felt alive, not dead, too.

My third day's training went like a blink of an eye:

9am–4pm full day. Full upgrade followed by focus on Mod1 training for first test – bike control, figure 8, U-turns, emergency stop, swerve etc.

It was more of the same repetitive training: stop between two cones with your front wheel, make the U-turn and pull up to the left-hand curb, swerve left and right at 30mph, emergency stop at 30mph when Shirley says stop, as well as the figure of eight, which needs to be completed three times consecutively.

The only new introduction to the training was to reverse the bike out at 180 degrees, then park it, which I managed with ease, even if I say so myself. The morning flew by and it was lunchtime before I knew it. We had even had time to grab a coffee in one of the local bike shops at mid-morning.

The best part of day three though, was when Shirley asked whether I would like to carry on with the practice by taking a ride out for an hour into the Suffolk countryside, including another stretch of the A14. Bit of a no-brainer really, as this was what I had been really looking forward to, opening up the bike a little and seeing the open roads, not just Ipswich town centre and all its council estates.

It was another bright sunny day, clear blue skies and a light breeze. Shirley got the A14 stretch out of the way first; back over the Orwell Bridge and then off on the Hadleigh road from Ipswich, turning off on the Hadleigh bypass to Bildeston, a famous village where the notorious Kray twins used to have a countryside retreat many years ago. It was then on through the backroads towards Needham Market and Ipswich, passing through the beautiful green countryside that really did look so pretty, with the wind in my ears and breeze running over the whole of my body. It was a great day and it finished all too soon for me. I really was enjoying this bike riding hobby.

It was now Day 4, and just one day to go before I had the Mod1 test:

> *9am–4pm full day. If Day 3 goes well, we will focus on Mod2 training – road riding, cover all junction types, road types, national speed limit etc.*

I knew in the back of my mind that if I failed the Mod1 test, it was game over for the week, and I would be looking at coming back later in the year to start all over again, as we were due to be in Spain for the summer and autumn.

It was off to the IRT off-road area first to spend an hour or so with a once-over of all the manoeuvres of the Mod1 test once again. I had a really good hour, with the exception of the U-turn, which I had been nailing each day previously. I carried out the manoeuvre three times and each time I just could not get the speed right, and once even placed a foot on the ground as I let my speed die and almost stalled. Shirley told me that if that was my test and I had put a foot on the floor it was an instant failure. It was a major fault if I hit a cone, or if I went too slow in the speed trap it would be a major, but one foot down during any exercise and it would be goodnight Lard Arse!

We set off for the next journey through the town, out to the ring road and heading towards the A14 once again. I had been so lucky with the weather all week, and it was a glorious day once again. That was four days running, and it was turning out to be the UK's best summer on record, and I had chosen this year to take my bike test. The Orwell Bridge was quite windy today and it really did feel like I was holding on for dear life. I had to lean sideways into the wind to brace myself from the gusts.

Out we went again into the Suffolk countryside, with Shirley instructing me on my road position as we rode. Something I really had no idea of until that day was that it is much more technical when you're riding and having to position yourself and the bike into the correct positions for right and left corners, as well as looking at the viewpoint and riding with your focus ahead of you, not looking at the front wheel, as my bad habits kept telling me to do. It was great though, and I felt like I was really learning fast, without being too over-confident. I was enjoying the ride out and feeling like I really had missed out over the past thirty-five years on a sport I had left behind once I passed my car test. Life going forward was going to be so much fun with two wheels now.

Today was my first time at the national speed limit too; only for one junction on the A14, due to the windy conditions, but it was clear to me I was not going to be a speed freak. I really enjoyed the bike, but 70mph did seem enough on the bike I was riding, especially in those conditions. Remember, it was all still new to me and I just wasn't comfortable going fast.

Once again, the day finished all too soon. Vanessa was there to collect me again, and then it was back for a rest and a final chill out before the following day's Mod1 test. Shirley was confident I would be okay, as I had shown great attitude in the learning and instruction. All I needed to do was get a good night's sleep and just enjoy the following day with confidence.

Test day for the Mod1 part of my licence. Escort to test centre for Mod1 test.

My test time was 11.30am. My day was to include a practice session on all the manoeuvres, then ride over to the test centre to be there by 11am to ensure I was registered with my papers, have a toilet break and then into the test.

The start of my practice period was at the IRT off-road area, and it was good, as I nailed each module, which really did my confidence the world of good. Shirley was not with me today as she had a personal appointment previously booked. Graham had been tasked with the job of escorting me around for the morning and to help get me over the line of the Mod1 test, so it was off for a quick ride around Ipswich and double-check my roundabouts once we left the practice area, before we headed to the test centre.

On arrival, I parked the bike facing forwards of the parking area on Graham's instruction, just to make sure I did not have to reverse and cause a problem prior to the test beginning. We went in and I booked in and handed over my licence and theory test etc. We were told to sit down and my examiner would call me through when he was ready.

The weather was great, mid-20s yet again, no wind and clear blue skies. I sat in the waiting area watching a young guy take his Mod1. He looked to be flying through the test and I just hoped I would be the same. Before long, the young guy had finished and I was called through to meet my instructor, Terry. He introduced himself. He looked slightly older than me and his whole attitude and the way he discussed the test with me was quite calming. I knew I was nervous, as I was cracking jokes just to ensure we both smiled or laughed. With the paperwork finished it was off to mount up and start the test.

Terry opened the gates to the test area, which was a tarmacked area, about the size of a football pitch, if not a bit bigger, with a large twelve-foot fence around it. There were cones already set out for each manoeuvre I had to carry out. Terry had first of all instructed me to just ride through the gates and pull up alongside him once he had finished opening the gates. Simple, that was my first instruction and carried out with no problem. I then waited until Terry closed the gates behind me for my next instruction, which was to wait where I was until he instructed me to move. I was then to ride over the test area to a group of four cones, then stop with my front wheel within the four cones. It was not an emergency stop, just purely pull up in full control of the bike in a given place.

It was only a minute or so wait until Terry was by the cones and I set off as instructed, pulled up with my front wheel within the four cones and awaited my next instruction. Terry then asked me to ride over to the other side of the test area to a set of eight cones that were marking out three parking areas. I was to ride over and park the bike within one of the parking areas of my choice, then await his arrival, as he would be walking behind me. I did this without a problem, my confidence growing, and it all felt so natural. Shirley had obviously done a great job of training me.

Terry then came over and instructed me to dismount the bike, reverse it into a different parking place, which he identified, then park the bike. Again I nailed it and the bike was parked without any problem. My next criteria would be the slow steady ride, with Terry walking alongside me. He gave the instruction on what he wanted and off we went. I was in full control and could just make out Terry in the corner of my eye. My speed was consistent and I pulled up twenty yards away as instructed. Another one nailed, my conscience was telling me.

Terry then instructed me to ride over to three cones in the far-right area of the test centre. I pulled up alongside the cones, then he instructed me to carry out a U-turn and pull up alongside a white line that was the marker to indicate a curb on the opposite side of the road. Terry moved over to the other side of the white line to view the manoeuvre. I started to release the clutch and the bike moved about two feet, but I had not used the throttle. I immediately stalled the bike and placed both feet on the ground to ensure the bike did not fall over and take me with it too.

My head went into full disappointment mode. I didn't look at Terry, as I didn't want to see what I knew was coming. I had grounded my feet on the floor. Yes, not just one foot, but both of them – instant failure. I counted to five, took a deep breath, and uttered a few choice words directed to myself. I was in control but wanted to carry on and finish the turn. Off I set again, and this time I nailed it, albeit one minute too late.

I apologised to Terry for the mistake once I pulled up next to the white line. He did not acknowledge my apology but instructed me to ride out to the next obstacle and carry out the figure of eight manoeuvre. My head was racing round with what had just happened. Disappointment is a word that cannot sum up how I was feeling. I was swearing away at myself on the inside for the mistake that would cost me not only the week's training, but another week's visit back to the UK to do it all again. More importantly, the Spanish and Portuguese trip was off again as I had put my foot on the bloody floor. I carried out the figure of eight as instructed. If I'm honest, that and the next two manoeuvres are a bit blurred, as I was so dejected after the disappointment of placing my feet on the floor.

The swerve to the right came next. It was the only one I was asked to do, and Terry had not instructed me to carry out the swerve to the left. I was now thinking that even he was fed up with the test, and he knew, just as I did, that I'd failed so he'd given up on getting me to do every part of it, but just wanted to get me out of the test area ready for the next person.

Finally it was on to the emergency stop. I did have to carry that out twice as I was only carrying 26mph when I went through the speed trap first time around. I did think it was pointless doing it twice, and in my head I was starting to get annoyed with myself and was muttering under my breath: "Terry, why bother with me doing it again? I've failed anyway." I carried it out a second time and Terry then instructed me to pull up in front of the entrance gates, where we could exit the test centre.

He opened the gates and instructed me to park the bike. I did, riding through the gates, parking the bike, and switching it off, swearing once again at myself, but telling myself I needed to thank him for his time. At least I had tried to do it first time, but I would just need a little more training. I removed my helmet and shook Terry's hand, thanking him for the test. I apologised for the mistake and started to walk away. Terry asked whether I would like to hear my test result now or wait and have a full debrief in his office. I told him he could give it now, as I knew what was coming.

As I was speaking, he said, "You will be glad to know your Mod1 is a pass." I asked him to repeat what he had just said. "You passed Martin."

"But what about my foot on the ground?" I asked. He then explained that a foot on the ground throughout most of the test would be an instant failure, but at the time and position it had happened to me, I was in full control of the bike. I did not panic, then I had carried out the manoeuvre with full control and no danger to me or any other road user.

The smile was all over my face as I walked into the test area, I thought Graham was expecting me to say it was a failure. I had done it, my Mod 1 was completed. I explained to Graham, who smiled and agreed it was a great result, as foot down normally meant failure, but occasionally, for a good reason as I hadn't moved away from side of 'road' it would only warrant a minor fault and still carried a pass.

We left the test centre and headed back to the IRT centre, where we had a cuppa and I was feeling elated. I remembered the feeling from my car test and passing first time after only a few lessons. At seventeen years old, it felt like a huge accomplishment, although this time I still had another test to do, but the feeling of elation was just the same.

Graham asked whether we should maybe take a ride out for a couple of hours and just get some ride time under my belt; just a bit of extra practice to build confidence. I agreed and jumped at the idea of another ride in the glorious sunshine in the Suffolk countryside. I knew I had a day off before my final Mod2 test and I could rest all day and enjoy it at my grandson's birthday party.

Then the final day came, and it really was D-Day for me, the Mod2, hopefully followed by the ride of a lifetime around the Iberian Peninsula, exploring the coast of Spain and Portugal.

Escort to test centre for Mod2 test.

I arrived as always at 8.30am and had a cuppa in the office. Graham was on a training day himself and Shirley was still away on personal business, so it was left to Clive, Graham's business partner to get me over the line. It sounds strange, three instructors during my six-day course, but it really was no problem. IRT really is a family and each of the instructors has good banter and really good clear instruction techniques, so once again I was in safe hands.

My test was again mid-morning, 10.30am this time. After a cuppa, we headed out just after 9am for a final run around the ring road and to practice my left and right junctions, roundabouts, and even a hill start or two, to build confidence. We headed back to the test centre office and arrived there for 10.15am, giving ample time to check in to the Mod 2, with my Mod 1 certificate, as well as my licence and theory certificate.

It was great news, as Terry walked through and called me up once again. He would be riding out with me for the Mod2, so immediately I felt a security blanket surround me, as I knew straight away this guy was honest. Not only would he be assessing my ability, but also my aptitude to carry out the instructions. Then he would issue an honest report and conclusion too, just as he had with my foot down issue, where he looked at the situation and gave an honest response, which for me resulted in a pass.

We rode through the town and also along the A14 during the test. My final section was to ride out to Manningtree, with no other instruction apart from that I was told I would be riding solo, with him following me and heading for Manningtree.

Mod2 was over so quick. I knew it was to last about forty minutes but it seemed only ten minutes later that we were heading into the test centre once again. The only issue I thought I had was right at the end when I forgot a life-saver look while turning into the test centre road. I parked the bike as I had done previously, by Clive's bike, turned the engine off and dismounted.

Unlike two days ago, today I had expectations. I was hoping all was well, and that after what I thought was an almost faultless ride I would pass. Terry walked over, having parked his bike, and we both removed our helmets.

"You will be happy to know, Martin, that you have achieved a pass for your Mod 2 motorbike test." He didn't wait to ask today, he just blurted it out at me. I had passed; I was now in possession of a full motorcycle licence. Dave would be just as happy when I got to tell him.

I walked back into the test centre with Terry, where I was debriefed on three minor faults I had made, although driving into the test centre was not one of them. I thanked Terry for his time, and he, in turn, humbly told me he had done nothing, and that I had passed the test, he had only observed and ensured I met the correct minimum criteria to ride a bike. He added that it was now down to me to ensure I took those skills and learned as much as possible over the coming years to hone them to ensure I became a good rider. What a great guy and a good lesson to learn as always. I might have the licence, but now I needed to learn how to ride by myself. If you're reading, Terry, I still thank you for the Mod1 pass, it was totally unexpected.

We returned back to the IRT for my last time, but this time I had the licence. Vanessa had been shopping in Ipswich all morning, waiting for me to finish early. It was 11.30am and I had time for a cuppa with Clive before Vanessa arrived to collect me at midday. I thanked Clive, and as I was about to leave, Shirley arrived just to see how I had done. She too was over the moon, thanked me for my custom and wished me all the very best for the future with my riding. I had already explained about my ride around the Iberian coast with Dave and she wished me a great journey and asked me to let her know how we got on.

It was goodbye now. Vanessa arrived and I set off with a huge smile and a great feeling of relief, as well as accomplishment. Lard Arse has his motorcycle licence ...

Chapter 4

Planning the Trip Around Spain & Portugal

Vanessa and I headed back to Spain two days after my test. It was a bad spring/early summer this year in Spain, and it had rained most of April and May. In fact, the weather was warmer in the UK at the time, which was a first. It was 22°C and cloudy but my mood was great.

Our next step would be to plan the route and decide how long the journey would take. Once we had managed that I would be able to then find a bike for the journey. I had already decided I would not buy one, as I needed to see just what kind of bike I wanted. The only thing I knew was that I must be comfortable. The Suzuki I had taken the test on was not the most comfortable bike. Graham and Shirley had both said I should try a touring bike, with good sitting position and easy riding, especially for my first journey.

I had to wait a few weeks to discuss the route with Dave as his wife had just taken early retirement from work and the two of them had gone off on a celebratory holiday around the USA and Canada. So, when early July came I was getting itchy to discuss the route with him, as I needed to find the right bike too.

After several emails, Dave suggested that we should just plan the first day and book our first overnight stay. Both Dave and I had worked out via Google and several navigation sites that we would be travelling between 4,000 and 4,500km, depending on any detours we would make.

Initially we had agreed that we would stay each night in bed and breakfast and plan each day the night before. I did, however, have an itch to get the tent out and have a few man-camping days too. Dave wasn't too keen to start with but, after a brief discussion, it was agreed that we would both be taking clothes etc. for five days only to save on space, so when we needed to wash our clothes we would camp and have a day off too. As all campsites, or the ones we would choose, would have the facilities to use their washing machines etc., if we searched well we could have a relaxing day off, get the washing done and enjoy the local sights in the area where we stayed each time.

Looking then at the journey and distance we would travel, Dave said it was his preference to not build up lots of kilometres each day but to travel only five or six hours daily, especially as he had a beginner with him. He also wanted to enjoy the journey and stop when he wanted to take a picture or drink a coffee, and generally just chill when the feeling took him. How could I argue? It sounded like Dave had the right idea. Let's face it, we were there to enjoy the ride not punish ourselves.

So with a minimum 4,000km to travel, we decided we would ride a maximum of 250km per day, which would give us a journey period of sixteen days, plus every fifth day free to wash our bits and recharge our batteries. So, in total we agreed twenty-one days, which also gave us an day extra just in case. It's not complicated really, but 250km is only 150 miles daily, and even if we did it at 60–65kph (40mph) we would be riding only four hours daily. This really was a nice pace and would also give us lots of time to explore. So the timing was planned and I could move on to find a bike.

With our other commitments we had already pencilled in September, but not before my granddaughter's birthday on the twelfth of the month. I was free from that day onwards. Dave would be travelling from the UK and taking the ferry to

Santander, then driving over two days to me at Marbella. He checked the ferry times etc. and booked the ferry for 11 September. He would arrive into Santander at about 7pm on the Wednesday evening, which meant he would take a bed and breakfast locally, then set off the next morning, heading to an overnight just south of Madrid. He would be arriving in Marbella early the next afternoon, Friday, 14 September. I wasn't happy that Dave would be doing so many hours solo, but he relished the fact that he had a solo stretch to do on his way to me as well as the way back.

So with Dave's ferry date booked we now agreed the start date would be early morning on Saturday, 15 September, with an end date of 5 October, twenty-one days later. Dave could then stay one night with me in southern Spain on our return, so we could get his washing done, then he would head back to get the ferry on the Sunday evening from Santander, arriving back in the UK early evening on Monday, 8 October. He is a three-hour ride from Southampton, so he would hope to be home around midnight. All sounded simple.

The final thing we needed to agree was which direction we would ride – clockwise or anti clockwise? The only thing I had niggling in the back of my head was that Portugal is on the Atlantic coastline. My thought was that it could be colder coming into autumn on the Atlantic coastline compared to the Mediterranean coast that dominated most of the Spanish coastline. Dave agreed that it might well be a factor so we agreed to travel clockwise on the journey.

I then suggested we both make a list of must-visit places on the journey, as Spain and Portugal have so many beautiful places and coastline towns and villages. Dave thought we should plan every day depending on the weather and our approximate distance, with a little give and take as to where to stay and what to visit. That way we had a focus every evening to do some research together, something that until now had not really happened, with us being in two different countries most of the time.

So that was the plan. The bulk of the journey would be planned en route. We would decide each evening just what we would set out to accomplish on the following day, where we would ride, and by what route.

Sounds easy – I just hoped it would turn out to be so simple!

Chapter 5

Finding a Bike

To most people, when taking on such a trip as we had organised, the bike is already in the garage and might only need a service and some minor adaptions. As you can see, I'm not like most people. I'd bitten off several challenges and commitments before I even thought of looking for a bike. But now was my time to look at the market and see just what was there for the period of time we had agreed.

I started with the hire shop in Fuengirola, which had originally offered me and Dave, two 125cc scooters to hire for four weeks at a price of €840. We both thought that was a great price, especially as it included breakdown cover and full insurance. I contacted Jac at the shop, who had originally emailed me the offer and arranged to visit them to see what options they had.

The shop was a Yamaha dealer too so my options were limited really to the Tracer 650cc, 900cc or 1200cc. I quickly ruled out the smaller bike as it gave me memories of the 125cc Kawasaki that I took out on the first day at Ipswich when I started my training. It just did not feel good. The 900cc was a good option and they changed the seat to a higher position. I sat and got the feel of it and it did feel really nice. I went through a few limited questions about the bike, which I as a novice had, and the bike did seem to tick all the boxes.

Moving on to the 1200cc model, again it looked and felt great. My only reservation was that I was new to this and was I asking for too much with the very top model? It was not a question I could answer so I asked Jac to send me an offer on both bikes. I explained our start and finish dates and reiterated the breakdown cover, where we were going and the approximate kilometres we would cover. Jac took all the details and assured me I would have the offer within forty-eight hours, which is exactly what happened. The basic offer had a difference of €10 per day, with the 1200cc bike being only a little more expensive. I thanked Jac and told him to hold the offer for a week or two whilst I made my decision.

My next move was to jump on to the internet and see just what else I could find. It was not easy, as I could not find what I was looking for in the search engines, as I was writing in English and getting results all over the English-speaking world, but not in my area of Spain. Google Translate came to the rescue though, and I started typing a few different searches into it for the Spanish translation, and soon enough I was looking at hire companies throughout my area in southern Spain. Jac's offer gave me a yardstick that I could use to see what bike and price I could get cheaper for my ride, but I would not let the quality of the machine suffer just to save a few euros.

I found an expat, Mark, only an hour or so away. It wasn't ideal but he dealt with BMW touring bikes. I knew nothing about them but I'm not proud, so I emailed the guy. I had a reply back within the hour, which is something I really like, an immediate response. I told him the whole story and what was happening, as well as the dates. The only thing was he did not think I should get the bigger bike he had there, the BMW R1200RT, and to be honest I would not have been happy either due to the size of the bike, just like the largest of the Yamahas. I agreed I would take a drive out the next Sunday, which was only a couple of days away, to look at the G650GS and the F800GS, both of which, Mark assured me, would be more than enough for my trip.

So, on the Sunday, Vanessa and I went out for a drive to investigate. The satnav said forty-four minutes but it ended up being an hour and ten. Mark met us at his home in the mountains, high on a plateau looking down on to some of the most stunning scenery in the southern Spanish regions. The position of the house was truly stunning, commanding the most spectacular panoramic views across the countryside with its rolling olive groves, to the mountains in the distance, where you could just make out the Embalses Guadalhorce-Guadalteba, a large reservoir that has been there for over a hundred years, surrounded by national park.

It was a short drive to Mark's garage, where he stored all the bikes that were for hire. Of the two bikes that were around my budget range, the F800GS and the G650GS were both in great shape but the G650GS realistically was not big enough for the trip; even Mark thought so. The F800GS was just over my budget, but only just, and did look man enough. Mark thought it was the ideal bike for the trip I had planned. I needed time to think though, but it was another option for me. I told Mark I would be in touch over the coming week to confirm my choice of bike. The bike was slightly over budget but it was also a long trip to collect it and redeliver after the trip, which would increase the cost and time on the bike that I would have to factor into the final decision.

I did, however, like the bike, and after discussing it with Dave, he informed me he had had the use of the same model earlier in the year when his had needed a service. He had used the F800GS for a little over a week in the end. So I set out to find the same model, if possible, closer to the area of Marbella. If I could find it closer it would make a big saving on time, and hopefully I could get a price that would be attractive too.

After a few hours searching I stumbled on a website advertising the very same bike, which was directly in Marbella, and their contact address showed they were only about fifteen minutes from my lodge. I had a brief discussion with them via email and it turned out that they would deliver the bike to me and collect it after I was finished too. The kilometre usage was unlimited and again breakdown cover was included, as well as being able to travel through any country in Europe. The price was also good; it was actually the cheapest of all the offers I had had. It was 20% cheaper than the Yamaha and almost 25% cheaper than the like-for-like hire from Mark with his BMW rental service.

The only problem I had was that I needed to see the bike. Call me old fashioned but if I'm going to spend money, I like to see what I'm spending it on, just as I had with the Yamaha Jac was offering me and the BMW with Mark. I took the address and set off the following day with Vanessa to find the shop/garage. The problem was that the address was a residential apartment house with no commercial outlets. I even tried two local shops close to the address and they had never heard of the company, and informed me that the address was an apartment in the residential building.

It didn't add up, so I called the number on their website and the guy spoke no English, so it was left to my broken Spanish to sort the problem out – no easy feat. What turned out to be too good to be true really was too good for me. The guy had a website and appeared to own three bikes, none of which could be viewed. The first time I would see it would be the day it was delivered. I also had to pay for the bike on reservation, something I really was not comfortable with. Again, I might have the complete wrong end of the stick here, but it just was not legitimate to my mind. I felt uncomfortable about the whole situation. He might have been a really genuine guy with a great business, but my conscience would not let me proceed with his terms, so I ruled him and his offer out.

I had a decision to make. I could keep trying to find something at a better price or deal with one of the two offers that were on the table already. I spoke to Dave once again but this time about the Yamaha Tracer 900. He took a look over a couple of days and told me that both bikes were good for the trip. The BMW he had had for a week's trial himself and could not fault it; the Yamaha had great reviews and it also had that little more PS, which would come in handy when we hit the mountainous regions, especially the Pyrenees, which Dave really was looking forward to.

I thanked Dave and now knew it was D-Day for the bike choice to be made. It was difficult but it really came down to travelling to collect the bike and then returning it. It just seemed pointless wasting half a day getting it and then again returning it when I had a bike on my doorstep and slightly cheaper than the BMW.

The decision was made, it was to be the Yamaha Tracer 900cc, so I emailed Jac. I did try to get the price a little cheaper but he wasn't having any of it. You can't fault me for trying though. Included in the rental price was two travel cases, each 35 litre and a rear box at 50 litre. I also asked for a 12v socket to be fixed to the bike for the days when we would be camping, so at least we had a fallback to be able to charge either the phones or satnav if needed. Jac said it was no problem and he would get it fitted to the bike in readiness for collection.

It was a great deal and I really was pleased. I booked the bike and also sent off the correct information, including a copy of my passport and driving licence, which were required for the hire. Jac confirmed within twenty-four hours and the bike was booked for collection on the morning of 14 September, with return date set for the afternoon of 5 October. We were ready now I had a bike, so all we needed to do now was watch the clock   tick   down   and   be   prepared!

Chapter 6

The Journey Begins

What a summer it had been. We were enjoying the heat of the Spanish summer in Marbella and we had both of Vanessa's parents out to visit us, which was a real pleasure. In all of that was the World Cup in Russia. Yes, England had finally come back to the world stage and, as a passionate football fan, it was my second World Cup semi-final and, yes, my second disappointment in going out. Hey ho ... as they say. I think we deserved the semi-final spot but the better team eventually won the game, even if I did get a lot of stick from an old Croatian work colleague from my time working in Germany in the 90s – well done Goran!

Mid-August saw our eldest son visit us with his family, which was a great week, with all the grandchildren around, and the weather was just perfect, clear skies, mid-30s and lots of swimming and fun for the children. It was all over too quick though, and before we knew it September had arrived and it was time for my final planning and preparation.

It was 11 September, and Dave was all ready to leave home. I had been messaged every other hour of the previous days, hearing all about what and how he was packing his bike in readiness to leave. I even had pictures of the bike fully loaded and heard all about his test rides around the Suffolk area to ensure the bike was all well balanced.

So here we go. Dave left around mid-morning on 11 September, heading for Southampton to get the ferry to Santander. I could feel my nerves mounting now. Remember, I was a complete novice and about to head off on a 4,000–5,000km bike ride, and I was feeling the strain. His ferry left on time at 5.30pm and, true to form, I received a picture of a pint of beer, as he sat in the bar once he had boarded and found his cabin. He was due to arrive in Santander the following day at 6pm. He was an hour late and, guess what, it was raining extremely hard – poor Dave!

It was no great hardship though, as he had booked a local B&B for the night in Liérganes, twenty minutes from the port, as he knew he was not going to be able to travel too much that day. So I received a few pictures of his evening meal and the hotel, as well as another beer or two in the local bar. Dave seemed just as excited as I was, and who could blame him? It seemed a long time since we had originally hatched the idea twelve months previously.

I was still very nervous. It was that bad that I was having to sit on the toilet every hour or so as my guts were tied up in knots. That's really not like me I must say, but I think it was taking me right out of my comfort zone, with the whole bike trip, and I knew I was nervous about collecting the bike and riding it back to get ready for Dave's arrival.

The following morning, 13 September, Dave messaged at about 9.30am to let me know he was just leaving the hotel. He had a 470km day of travelling ahead of him to get to the town of Tembleque, approximately 40km south of Madrid. I was still not happy that Dave was on his own travelling and, secondly, I needed my stomach to calm down. I was really not myself. Dave messaged a couple of times on his journey through the day but it was only 4pm when he finally messaged to say he had arrived at his hotel for the night. No dramas and he was safe and sound, with the obligatory picture of a beer on the table for me to look at.

Tomorrow was to be the penultimate day of my waiting. Friday 14 September, and Dave messaged early to let me know he was fine and leaving at around 9am. I wished him good luck and said to keep in touch again on his travels. I had a full morning planned. First I had to get off the toilet; yes, I was still very nervous and it was really affecting me. I had the bike to collect, and Vanessa and I were driving into downtown Marbella to meet Jac and to finalise the rental in his Marbella shop. Vanessa would then drive the car back to the lodge and I would follow on my first solo ride on a bike since passing my test. The worrying thing for me was that the stretch of the A-7 main highway we lived on was an absolutely crazy road. I can only describe it as one of, if not the worst road in Europe, with idiots driving twenty-four hours a day on it and always overcrowded.

I was at the shop for 10am as arranged, just as they opened. Jac had everything ready, we quickly sorted the paperwork and the money out, and Jac gave me a full once-over on the bike. He brought the bike from the lower level of the shop up to the front of the shop, where it would be easier for me to get back on to the A-7 and head home.

The bike looked great, petrol blue with two brand-new suitcases and rear box. I was so nervous that I was unable to do up my jacket. Yes, I felt like a real plonker, all fingers and thumbs. I eventually got myself together and managed to sort out how to use the zip on my jacket. Jac wished me good luck and disappeared inside. He must have realised I was nervous and thought it best to just leave me to it. With a deep breath I pulled in the clutch, put my foot on the brake and hit the start button. The bike fired up and this was to be the start of my biking career.

******

Dave had approximately 420km to ride today. By the time I made it back to the lodge it was just after 11.30am, and he would have been approximately halfway, as we were expecting him about 3pm if all went well.

Arriving back at the lodge I felt like a weight had been lifted off me. The bike was great, I had had no problems riding it back, and that felt so good inside. My stomach was even starting to feel better too. All I had to do now was pack everything on to the bike and make sure I had enough room in the suitcases and rear box. Jac had even given me a travel net free of charge just in case I needed it. I was like a child in a sweet shop, messing around the bike and packing, unpacking and repacking to get the weight good on both the left and right and ensure I didn't forget anything. I had no worries, as I had so much space I could even pack the tent and mattress in the suitcases so that everything was dry and locked up at all times while we travelled.

Vanessa and I had a late lunch after I had finished loading the bike and Dave messaged to say he was just outside Malaga, only about forty-five minutes away. It was 2.15pm and he had had no problems on the way down so far. I did warn him, though, that we were due a heavy thunderstorm that afternoon and the skies were not looking good at that moment either. It was very dark and the wind was getting up too.

It was forty-five minutes later that we heard again from him. He was just outside a campsite in Cabopino, approximately 5km away. The storm had hit him and he was seeking shelter in a Shell garage until it cleared. I told him to message when he left and I would drive down in the car to the main A-7 road and keep an eye out for him, so he could then follow me back to the lodge.

It was actually only ten minutes before he messaged. He arrived okay, not too wet either. Vanessa straight away got stuck in to washing his dirty clothing, as he had been on the road since Tuesday and it was now Friday. Dave chilled for an hour and then we started organising last minute details. Firstly, we had to fit the two intercom systems we had bought into our helmets to enable us to chat whilst riding. The intercoms were cheap Chinese ones at €40 each, but they looked great and fitted into both helmets fine. We tried them out once we had sussed out how they worked and the clarity of the sound was fantastic.

Dave was impressed with the bike and it wasn't long before we popped out together. Dave's excuse was he wanted to check the intercoms whilst we rode, but I think he was taking a look at me on the bike and my riding skills! Either way it was fine. We popped out for thirty minutes just to say we had checked everything and were soon back at the lodge.

We walked down to the local bar in the early evening and had a couple of beers, then out to a local pizza restaurant for dinner. We were in bed by 10pm and ready for the start of the journey in the morning.

******

Saturday, 15 September
29°C – clear skies with thunderstorm late afternoon
178km travelled today

It was 6.45am and Vanessa was already up and dressed. I was running her to the airport in Malaga as she was going on an African safari with her best friend Wendy. We left for the airport at 7.30am; I was eager to get back and Vanessa was excited to be travelling on a dream holiday of her own. I dropped her off and we wished each other good luck and a safe holiday. It would be three weeks before we were back together. As I left I could feel the excitement mounting in me too. This was to be the start of what I hoped would be a safe and fantastic experience on two wheels.

I was back at the lodge by 9.30am, just enough time for a cuppa and a slice of toast. Dave was up and well organised. He had spoken with Caroline and she too had sent best wishes to the two of us. By now it was 10.30am, time for a final check over the bikes, to make sure everything was locked on and securely fixed. Dave had his tent fixed down with a net over his back seating area and two suitcases on the bike. I locked up the lodge, we synced the helmet intercoms, and we were ready to go. As we pulled out I waved to our neighbour Tommo, who had been waiting for our departure, then we were off.

I was leading to start with, as we had to get through the Marbella traffic on the A-7 without hitting the toll road. So we hit the road, cruised around Marbella and up towards Estepona. Traffic was not too bad so we could keep an 80–90kph speed going, which if you know the area is quite good for this road.

Before too long we were past Estepona and still on the A-7, heading down towards San Luis de Sabinillas close by to Puerto de la Duquesa; yes, the same port we had visited the year before on Dave and Caroline's visit to us in Fuengirola. The weather was with us at the time, clear blue skies and sunny, although there was a forecast of thunderstorms again by mid-afternoon.

We stopped by the coast in Sabinillas for a coffee. We had only been on the road for just over an hour but, as we had originally said, it's a journey to enjoy not a chore. We were heading down to the most southerly point in Europe, Tarifa, a beautiful Moorish costal port with a huge kite surfing beach, over 7km long, and it must be 200m deep, and almost always empty except for the kite surfing dudes.

I was still nervous and, although I had no problem with the bike, I was still tiptoeing around the few roundabouts we came across, and overtaking was not something I was too confident with either. We didn't have too long though, as just before Tarifa there was a viewing point to the right, directly off the A-7. We pulled in to a car park full of twitchers and holidaymakers enjoying the view.

We parked up and walked up to the high point, which had a low-level wall around the viewing point. The view was stunning. We must have been 300–400m above the town of Tarifa, which was about 3km away to our left, and we could look down on to it. The beach stretched away into the distance to our right, and the A-7 was between us and the beach, weaving away along the coastline into the distance. Out to sea you could see the coastline of Africa. It was a little hazy, so the view was not fantastic, but when it's only 14km away you're always going to get a great view of the coastline, especially having such a great vantage point as we had.

Looking around you could also see why so many twitchers were present at the top of a dusty track to the right of the parking area. Crowded under what looked like a bus shelter were about fifteen to twenty people, mostly dressed in khaki and walking shoes, and equipped with state-of-the-art telescopes and camera lenses. I was wondering who or what they were all looking at. It could easily have put the most veteran paparazzi to shame.

It was quiet, then I noticed everyone scanning the sky. It was mostly blue, with a few wisps of cloud and not much else. But then, out of nowhere they appeared. Suddenly, all cameras and binoculars pointed upwards, and there was tangible excitement in the air. It looked like today was going to be a good one for this crowd. Forming circles above us and over the vast surrounding area in the sky were booted eagles, short-toed eagles, black kites and honey buzzards. Don't think I'm the expert at naming these birds, as at the time I had no idea what they were, but with a little research once home, I could easily work out that the most dominant birds in the sky on that day were the honey buzzards and black kites.

It was obviously a huge attraction to the onlookers, as the place really was humming. It was all over too quick though, and we were back on the bikes, heading just a short way up the coast to a small village called Bolonia, or Baelo Claudia as it was known in Roman times. Only 15km from Tarifa, this stop was to be our dinner break.

We arrived and headed for the car park that was signposted. Little did I know this was to be a small challenge in itself. As we approached the entrance, we found it was a dirt track that had a short 5–6m steep – very steep – rise to it. As I rode in I didn't realise it would need more power and I stalled the bike. Luckily I hit the hand brake and rested my feet on the ground. I did, however, have to roll back gingerly to get a second run up at it, and this time around I made it up, albeit a little embarrassed. We parked up and sat down in one of the local café beach restaurants for lunch. I then explained to Dave just where we were.

Baelo Claudia is one of most significant and well-preserved Roman archaeological sites on the Iberian Peninsula. The extensive ruins are situated on the Costa de la Luz, also renowned for its beautiful beach. The site´s important history rests on the former city having been a strategic point for trade routes between Europe and North Africa close by. The entrance to the Straits of Gibraltar are just 14km wide at their narrowest point, and Baelo Claudia profited from its proximity. The remains of the impressive temple, forum, basilica, baths, aqueduct and large fish-salting factory in particular, can all be explored today, giving an insight into the former glory of the city. Unfortunately we did not have the time to explore the ruins in great depth as we were on a schedule, but if you're ever in the region, it's free to get in and there is a tourist centre there that I can vouch for as being very interesting, and the parking at the centre is also free.

It was about 3pm when we left Bolonia, and we headed back to the main road, which by now was the N-340. It was only a kilometre or two before we were now on to a single-lane road but very good quality, as almost all roads are in Spain. Within twenty minutes we were turning left again on to the A-2227, a small country road that would lead us to our first night's accommodation. We were now chasing the clear skies, as just as we turned left on to the A-2227, there was a storm cloud awaiting us and we were very close to the deluge it was dumping over the area.

The road was good but quite windy and it had already rained here as the road was damp. We had about 10–12 km to go before we arrived at La Finca Palmeras in the village of La Zarzuela. The wind was getting even stronger and we were both urging each other on, as we knew the rain would be here any minute.

As we rode into the village the rain started, and instead of looking for our accommodation, Dave spotted an old derelict building with a parking area next to it where we could get shelter from the rain, so be both pulled over, parked pretty sharply, and took cover. Dave took his phone out and, with the use of Google Maps, found that we were only 500m away from the accommodation. We waited only five to ten minutes for the rain to die down, then Dave called the guy he had booked the room with and we arranged to meet in five minutes, so we headed straight for it.

The guy spoke very little English, so it was up to me to use the limited Spanish I had learned during the past two months just for the holidays. We got by and the guy showed us to our room, which was in an outside block of three small double rooms, each with a shower room inside. We were a bit damp from the rain, so decided to strip down and dry out. I asked the guy if he had Wi-Fi and he said yes, and that he would ensure it was switched on.

The strangest thing happened then. He went and got his ladder and shinned up on to the roof. He then shouted down to ask whether the Wi-Fi was good. It was now working, but why he had to go up to the roof I had no idea. He also pointed us to a place to eat in the evening, which was only a ten-minute walk away. We chilled out, I made some notes in my journal of the day's events, then had a shower and changed ready for the evening.

We walked back to the main road, crossed it and headed towards the restaurant. The first thing we came to was a local bar/restaurant called El Pollo, which translates as The Chicken in English. We decided to pop in and have a beer, as the place looked lively. I ordered two small beers and we went outside to people watch. It really was a locals bar. On a table opposite us was a young girl of about fourteen or fifteen years old, who had a small queue of four ladies, all in their thirties or forties waiting to have their nails painted by the youngster – and this was all in the outside area of the bar. Several of the locals were getting rowdy over a Malaga football game on the TV but

I could not see who they were playing or the score. It didn't sound too encouraging though, as there were plenty of groans coming out.

We had another beer, then decided to head over to the restaurant. It was only a five-minute walk from El Pollo. We entered the restaurant/bar, called Venta a Los Cuatro Vientos, where there was a really nice young man behind the bar who spoke a little English. We ordered two beers and asked for the menu. The beers came out but no menu, so I asked again and was told they were not open for food. Bugger, and this place was recommended too. He explained that there was a pizza bar only ten minutes away that would be open, but not until 8pm. It was 7.10pm by this time, so we decided to have a couple of beers there and the guy brought out some knick-knacks for us to nibble on.

At 7.45pm three women walked in and started opening the kitchen up, cleaning down the service area, and one started setting the tables in the bar for food. I asked the guy if they were opening up, to which he replied, "Yes, we open at 8.30pm." Then one of the ladies came over, who spoke great English, and apologised that the kitchen would not open until 9pm as they were running late, and she bought us a beer on the house too. So, after the confusion of whether they do or don't serve food on a Saturday evening, we were to be eating here tonight, and with the beer flowing we settled back and discussed the first day.

Dave had a fish dish and I ordered a pork belly dish, both of which were outstanding. There was a reason this place had a good name. All too soon it was time to leave, and not too soon either. Whilst we had been waiting for the kitchen to open, Dave had booked our following day's accommodation in Tavira, just inside the Portuguese border. It was a long ride in the morning, with a full day visiting several places of interest on the way.

Chapter 7

Day Two – Blessed on My Way to Our Pilgrimage at El Rocío

Sunday, 16 September

34°C – clear skies

517km travelled today

We were up and showered by 8am, waiting for breakfast that was due to be served at 9am. We were the only guests in the place so we decided to walk over to the breakfast area and sit down. We were in luck, as coffee was ready and service took another five minutes for the hard-boiled eggs to arrive, with a roll and a couple of slices of bread. It was nice, and we agreed that the first night's accommodation was a success.

By 8.45am we were on the road, all fully loaded and excited for another great day's adventuring ahead. With clear blue skies and a morning temperature of 19°C as we left, it was going to be a great day.

We headed for the coast, which was only 4km away, for the very small village of Zahara de los Atunes, and from there we headed north on the A-2231 coast road, following the signs for Conil de la Frontera. The ride was a real spectacle. For most of the first hour, we were only ever 200m from the sea, following the coastline and enjoying the wonderful views. I had a real surprise coming for Dave, as by 9.30am we would have our first stop, at Trafalgar, famous for the Battle of Trafalgar.

Using the intercoms was making life very easy for us both to follow each other, and we had worked out that as long as we stayed within 500–600m of each other and at a speed of no more than 110kph, we could speak and hear each other really well. It was also my security blanket as a beginner on the bike too, but Dave was really good at encouraging me every moment he could. The coast road ride was really picturesque, the sea was quite calm and there was not a soul in sight on this Sunday morning.

It wasn't long before we were finding our route through the fishing town of Barbate, or as it's known locally, Barbate de Franco, because General Francisco Franco spent leisure time there during his reign. Barbate, just like Bolonia the day before, has a long history of fishing stretching back to Roman times, when fish salting was at its peak.

Today there was a small fleet of fishing boats in the harbour, some of which were there for the tuna fishing. Tuna are found off this coast during the months of April through to September, when they enter the Mediterranean via the Straits of Gibraltar to spawn. We were through the town within ten minutes and our first stop was only another 14km away.

Arriving at Trafalgar is quite a low-key adventure. It is famed for the battle fought by the British Royal Navy against the combined fleets of the French and Spanish navies during the Napoleonic Wars. The battle involved twenty-seven British ships, led by Admiral Lord Nelson aboard *HMS Victory*, who defeated thirty-three French and Spanish ships under the French Admiral Villeneuve. This battle took place on 21 October 1805 just off Cape Trafalgar. It was during this battle that Nelson was shot by a French musketeer and died shortly before the battle ended. The rest, as they say, is etched into British history, and both Nelson and *HMS Victory* are now national treasures.

We turned left on to the small tarmac road leading to the beach areas. The village itself sits both sides of the main road and has several hostels and camping areas. As we rode down toward the beach and coastline, there were many locals setting up their stalls selling all sorts of bits, ranging from the normal beach wear to hats and cold drinks – nothing too exciting.

At the end of the road is a small roundabout with a bar across it blocking access to the road leading up to the lighthouse on the high cliffs above Cape Trafalgar. We parked the bikes to the right of the roundabout, but we decided not to walk up to the lighthouse, as it is over a kilometre away, and as the temperature was rising and we were in our biking gear, we settled for a few pictures before moving on.

It was for me a surreal feeling, as it always is when I visit Trafalgar, being in the place where such a huge historic event took place in British history, and I must say it is an absolutely beautiful beach area too. I have in the past made the walk to the lighthouse and the views both north and south over the cape are really awesome and well worth the hour or so to walk there and back.

Time to leave, and we headed back up the road, dodging the few holidaymakers that were now starting to appear. We hit the main road again and were still going north, heading for Conil de la Frontera. We passed through the surf dude coastal village of El Palmar, a typical dude place with loads of VW campers parked along the coast road and many surfers in the water or hanging out on the beach. One day I'm sure I will visit the village for a weekend to see what the fuss of surfing is all about.

We were now heading up to Conil and we had originally said we would stop for a coffee there as I love the town. I've been there several times and it's not a tourist town for the likes of expats, as it's a traditional Spanish holiday seaside town. It's full of fantastic tapas bars and has a lovely café culture. Walking through this small town is an experience, and I dare anyone to say it is not lovely.

Today though, we had changed our minds. We discussed it over the intercoms as we approached the town and decided that as we had such a long day ahead of us, it was best to keep moving, as it was already 11am and we also needed fuel soon, so we carried on.

We picked up the N-340 once again, now heading for Cadiz. We would not be stopping there either but had to ride around it in the direction of Seville. We then skirted around Jerez and pulled over in a service station to refuel, as we were both getting low now, having travelled over 300km since we left the day before. We filled up and had a quick chat about stopping shortly along the route for a coffee, as we had been on the road for two and a half hours by now. We left the petrol station and, as we hit the roundabout, Dave told me to let him past, as he would lead until we found a town or village for coffee. He led off and I was talking away to him, but no answer was coming back. Maybe he just had the hump, so I let it go.

Ten minutes later I asked Dave over the intercom yet again whether we were stopping, as we had passed two coffee shops in the past few miles, but again no answer. I decided to turn my volume up. Well the thought was there but I was then in a little panic as I could not find the intercom unit, which should have been on the side of my helmet. I searched and searched with my left hand but it was not there. I was gutted, not that I could not actually speak to Dave, but I knew, as I'm sure he did too, that the intercom was my small safety blanket as a beginner, and hearing Dave and his small tips as I learned to ride was to me invaluable.

I pulled alongside him and instructed him to pull over. Two minutes later we were in a parking area and I let him know what the problem was. We headed back to the garage and doubled back on our tracks, trying to find the unit but we could not. I was feeling quite deflated now and in need of the coffee we had planned.

We headed off and twenty minutes later stopped in the town of El Cuervo de Seville. The place was very busy but we managed to park right outside a nice little coffee shop and find a table to sit down at. The waiter came over and we ordered coffee and a water. The temperature was now up to 28–29°C, with clear sunny skies.

Dave started winding me up about the intercom but I must admit, for such a simple little item, I was gutted and I felt quite naked. Never mind, I needed to man up, as we had a great experience ahead of us now as we were going to ride past Seville and then on to El Rocío, a small town in the Spanish national park of Doñana.

Coffee over, and we were back on the road. It was about forty-five minutes before we rode around the outskirts of Seville, then north west towards Portugal. It is on the main exit/junction between the SE-30 and the autovia A-49 that there is a 270-degree exit with a very tight turning circle to the left. Dave was in front and I was trying to keep him about 100–150m ahead of me for when we hit the exit to the junction. On such a tight corner I could not see him and he couldn't see me either. I slowed down and started fine as I entered the corner. My problem was I just could not get the bike to go left. Thinking back, I was probably trying too hard with the reverse steering and pushing the handle bars the wrong way.

You can imagine what happened next. I hit the armour fencing on the side of the exit, but thankfully I stayed on the bike. I had hit it at such an angle that I had also squashed my right foot and clipped the front of the bike. Thankfully there was no one behind me, and I managed to ride on, but the short sharp shock had woken me up. I managed to slow the bike right down and get it back in the right direction. Thank god someone must have been looking down on me that day.

I got on to the main carriageway and could see Dave out in front. We carried on, as there was no point in stopping to tell him, as I was okay. I could check the bike when we arrived at El Rocío.

By the time we arrived at El Rocío it was 2.45pm. We had so far today travelled 305km and had almost the same to do once our visit here was over. El Rocío is Spain's strangest town. Nestled on the edge of the wild lagoons and the marshes of Doñana National Park, the town looks like a film set from a spaghetti western. You really would be forgiven for thinking that Clint Eastwood might emerge from one of its bars or cafés, unhitch his horse and ride off down the town's sandy streets. So why did we stop here? Well it was my Spanish teacher who had said it's a must-see town and explained why.

El Rocío is the annual pilgrimage at Pentecost. The Romería del Rocío is one of Spain's biggest festivals, when this small town's population swells from seven hundred people to something four times the size of Glastonbury. Yes, nearly a million people descend on the town to honour the saint and enjoy the party atmosphere. I've been told that it can get pretty insane and hedonistic, with lots of drunken behaviour, more appropriate to a clubbing weekend or stag night in Ibiza. It's such a famous event now that the fiesta's fame has grown to such an extent that the event is even broadcast on Spanish TV.

But why were we here in El Rocío? What is the attraction? Well, the short story is that in the 13th century, a local shepherd, over two miles from his home, noticed a figurine of the Virgin Mary in a tree. With the Moors ruling the region and Catholicism banned, he took the figurine down and headed home to hide it in his home. On his way home he felt tired and decided to have a short siesta. He laid down and covered the Virgin Mary, waking an hour later to find her gone. He was worried, so he retraced his steps back to the tree where he had found her. To his amazement the figurine was back in the tree, as high up as she had been earlier when he had found her. It was a miracle! He returned home and told of the miracle and the story of what happened.

Eventually a cathedral was built to house the figurine and it has over the years become a place of pilgrimage for the

Spanish, as well as Catholics from all over the world. If you're ever in the Seville area and want a great day out, take a bus or drive down to El Rocío. It's a great place and well worth the visit.

We headed back to the bikes after a coffee and some fluids, as the heat really was getting at us in our biking gear. We left El Rocío at about 3.45pm and we still had 250km to go. It was on the way back to the bikes that I realised that when we had discussed the distance we would travel today, Dave was talking in miles and I was thinking in kilometres, which is how we ended up with our longest day on the road, doing over 320 miles or more than 500km. This wouldn't be happening again as I was knackered, especially after my scare earlier in the day.

We decided we would head back to the main autovia and stay with it rather than take the B-roads, as even on them we would be travelling another two to three hours.

We stopped just over the river Guadiana, the border of Spain and Portugal, to refill with fuel once more. We were now only twenty to twenty-five minutes away. To our left was the Castro Marim golf club, where I have played a few times over the years when travelling with my good friend Tom O'Brian and his Irish golf society, and their annual world cup was played on this coastline.

We were only a kilometre or so from the coast as we travelled the short distance to Tavira. Finding the hotel was a little tricky, as we had to go through the old town. With very narrow streets, with the old white-washed buildings and cobbled roads, it wasn't easy, but we eventually found the hotel and checked in.

I was exhausted. Even thinking about my close call today and my near accident made me nervous but at least Dave was taking the piss and trying as he could to cheer up the situation, especially as on top of all of this I had no intercom now. I would have to try to sort it out soon, I thought, but not at the moment. First we needed food.

The hotel was a fifteen-minute walk down into the town of Tavira, a lovely town sitting on the river Gilão, where it meets the Atlantic Ocean. Again, this town was one of the Moorish main settlements of the region, and today there is much evidence of this, with a lovely old town and a real Moroccan feel to areas of it.

We headed over the river and into the town square, where we found many restaurants. There was a huge choice, but really it came down to where we could find a seat. The first restaurant we found with a free table was an Indian, so it was to be a curry and a couple of beers to start our journey through Portugal.

It was hot and muggy, but it was nice to relax after what was for me a hard day, with too many miles on the clock. We decided that in future we would not book our accommodation until we stopped at lunchtime as we travelled, so that we could measure just how we both felt each day and how far we wanted to push on without being too tired as we were today.

We ordered one more beer and sat people watching as we both spoke via WhatsApp to Vanessa and Caroline to let them know we were okay. It was past 9.30pm now and we walked through the town again, just mooching back to the hotel and a well-deserved night's sleep.

Chapter 8

Through the Algarve to Meet Our New Twitcher Friends

Monday, 17 September

34°C – clear skies

291km travelled today

Breakfast was to turn out to be our staple diet or main meal of the day, and this hotel was just fantastic. The Hotel Don Rodrigues set a very high benchmark for the rest to follow, especially the Portuguese custard tarts, or Pastéis de Nata, as they are called locally; still warm, and we just could not get enough of them.

We checked out of the hotel with a plan to have coffee in an hour or two, and if we came across any bike shops we would pop in to see if we could maybe sort out the intercom problem I had caused.

The route was not like the previous two days, as the whole of the Algarve seemed totally commercial and in my opinion not the most beautiful place to be. En route we passed the Algarve Aquaworld, which I can tell you now might give the little ones lots of fun but it looked totally run down and really uninviting. We did not have the nice scenery around us during the morning, as it was very over-developed and we spent most of the first three hours travelling at 50–65kph, hitting roundabouts every two miles. Even though this was great practice for my riding skills, to be approaching and attacking so many roundabouts, it became very boring all too soon.

Just outside Albufeira we took a short stop at a Yamaha garage, the first bike shop we had seen, just on the off chance they might be able to assist with the intercom. Although they did have some intercoms in stock, at €272 each, I was soon back on the bike without one.

The weather was getting warm now so we decided to pop into Albufeira for a coffee and a much needed cold water, as the heat and slow-moving traffic was making our body temperatures go sky high. We slowly made our way down the very steep and narrow roads to the waterfront area and parked the bikes in the high street that ran along the beach front.

There was a local market on and people everywhere, so parking the bikes was not an easy manoeuvre. We didn't mooch about too much as we both needed a cold drink, so we sat down at the first café and ordered two Americano coffees and two sparkling waters. The water came first, and by the time the coffee was brought over, we ordered two more waters as we were still thirsty.

We spent thirty minutes people watching as it was still busy and it did seem to be mostly English people walking through the market along the high street. We asked for the bill and paid. At €13 for two coffees and four small waters this place was by far the most expensive pitstop we would have throughout our whole journey.

Back on the bikes we gingerly made our way back up the tight roads and cobbles, making our way back to the main N-125, heading for the town of Sagres at the very tip of the Portuguese Algarve. We rode down on to the bypass that took us around Largos and within the hour finally got to see the coast again, even if it was only for ten minutes before we were pushed back a mile or two inland. Off past Praia de Luz and then Budens, it had been a very uneventful morning, with nothing but overpriced coffees and more roundabouts than you can imagine. The afternoon must be better!

As we approached Sagres there was a small village just off the main road, Vila do BPO, right on the junction where we were to start heading north towards Lisbon. Thankfully the last twenty minutes had seen us finally getting into less populated areas and the village of Vila do BPO really was on its own in the middle of nowhere.

The village has a steep hill with the oldest cobbles you could imagine. These stones had not been repaired for decades and they were awful to ride over, like riding along with a full speed industrial Kango drill on my lap. Parking in the small market place and eventually getting the bikes to stand without the risk of them falling over, we headed for the only café/shop about.

It was noon by now and neither of us was hungry after the breakfast we had eaten but we were both dehydrated again, so coffee and water it was. The young waiter spoke great English and we sat there for thirty minutes just taking in the day so far and chilling out as we watched the local life go by. Most of the village did look run down but in a nice way. I don't think there was anything I would have changed in it. It was what you could only imagine this village had looked like for a hundred years, and well worth a visit.

Hitting the road, we were now heading north on the N-268. We were not going to see the coastline for most of the day, as the closest road to the coast ran about three or four kilometres inland; however, we did have the pleasure of riding for the first time on the trip into some lovely countryside and along lovely roads. We stopped two or three times over the next three hours just to take the scenery in and take a few pictures of the journey.

The day was turning into a great one, and with little or no traffic en route, I was enjoying it even more. Dave sped off once or twice into what he called the 'twisties' – sharp corners. There was an abundance of them followed by open road and topped with great scenery. I, however, had work to do practicing my reverse steering and building my confidence back again after yesterday's mishap. I didn't mind being left, it was Dave's journey just as much as mine, and as he is the experienced rider, he needed to get out and enjoy the moments when they came along. It was a partnership starting to build and I felt we were both enjoying the afternoon.

Soon we entered huge open plains, very flat with small sections of tree-lined forests here and there that reminded me of Thetford Forest back in East Anglia. Just before the town of Odemira, we turned left to get back towards the coast, taking the N-393. The afternoon's ride was a real pleasure, no chasing kilometres, just pure enjoyment.

As we approached the town of Vila Nova de Milfontes we could see the huge estuary and the bridge that spanned it. To our left as we rode over it you had tree-lined waterfronts, the estuary mouth and the Atlantic behind it. Above the right-hand side of the estuary mouth was the town of Vila Nova de Milfontes itself, visible only by the white-washed buildings and terracotta rooftops. As we crossed the bridge there was nothing but tree-lined banks left and right as the river Mira meandered into the distance, with mountains filling the skyline after that. We stopped for a couple of pictures and just to take in the moment.

So off we went again. Now we were heading for Sines, a very small town below the Lisbon estuary. Dave had found a great hotel at a great price 20km or so north of Sines and with a supermarket next to it. Both of us fancied something simple today after last night's Indian and a huge breakfast.

The scenery was great for the next hour as we skirted along the N-125 again en route. We rode around Sines and hit the signs for Vila Nova de Santo Andre, and the Hotel Rural Monte Da Lezíria. We arrived just after 5.30pm. It was still hot and we checked into a ground floor twin room. Again Dave had done a great job in booking a lovely hotel, and the girl on reception spoke great English and had some really good customer service skills.

Dave showered first and I headed back to reception for a chat with the receptionist. I had thought maybe I could get a new intercom via Amazon, so I discussed the whole story with the young lady and she was kind enough to take a look on Amazon for me. She could find them, but my problem was I only had a Spanish account with Amazon. She explained it would be easier if I bought a new device in Spain and did what was described as a click and collect. I had it all explained to me, and as soon as we were in Spain I could organise a new intercom and collect it en route. That did make me feel a little better, especially as I had asked Dave to buy one too, and after the first day he wasn't able to use his either.

Back in the room, Dave popped out to the terrace for a chat with Caroline and I showered and cleaned myself up. After a quick change I placed all my bike gear outside to freshen up, as I had been sweating all day and the suit was quite damp, as were my boots. I messaged Vanessa and wished her good luck, as she was to be travelling the following day to Africa on her safari with her friend Wendy. Then it was off out for dinner.

We spoke to the receptionist once again and she told us the quick route to the supermarket. It was only a ten-minute walk and it was good to stretch our legs on the way over there. Surprisingly, the supermarket was huge in comparison to the size of the town we were in. It even had a hot food section at the back, just by the meat counter. The rotisserie chicken looked lovely and we didn't need asking twice. It was chicken and a roll for dinner, so off we went back to the hotel with a couple of chickens, with plans to eat on the terrace in the evening sun.

We entered the hotel and the receptionist asked if we found the supermarket okay, and we explained that we had and that we were to have a lovely roasted chicken each for dinner. She smiled and asked if we would like to eat in the bar. We didn't know there was a bar. She asked us to follow her upstairs and there was the bar, empty but it was a lovely area to eat and have a beer with our dinner. We ordered two beers, Super Bock, cold and very nice.

The receptionist left us and we tucked into dinner. It was a lovely change not to be eating in a restaurant, and this after only three days. We ordered another beer and finished off dinner. We were both stuffed, and as we finished, two elderly guys entered the bar. They asked if we were the owners of the two bikes in the car park, as they had noticed Dave's registration plate said it was from a Nottinghamshire dealer. Dave explained that the plate came with the bike when he bought it but he was from Suffolk, not the shires.

We all introduced ourselves and it transpired that our two new friends, Peter and John, had been visiting the same hotel for over twenty-five years. They were birdwatchers, yes twitchers, but they were not just watching birds, they were here to help with the local Natural Reserve of the Lagoons of Santo André and Santa Sancha. For over twenty-five years they had been coming here as a party of nature lovers to assist in the counting of wildlife migratory birds, as well as help with the general maintenance of the reserve walkways and boardwalks as needed by the park rangers. That day and for the next two days they were ringing birds first thing in the morning and last thing in the evening. It was very interesting listening to some of their stories and they both had a huge knowledge of the area we were in and the surrounding areas.

We then got on to the subject of the journey we were on, where we had started from, what we expected to see and where we were travelling to over the coming weeks. Both guys thought we were going to have a real fun time on our journey, and were very enthusiastic for us. Peter asked if we were taking the ferry in the morning into Lisbon. What ferry, we wondered?

Peter explained there was a ferry about 50km north from where we were, at a place called Troia. It crossed the estuary towards Lisbon, and took only about thirty minutes, so would save us at least three hours riding time. Dave immediately started searching Google for the Troia ferry. The guys were correct, the ferry dock was about 50km north on a very thin spit going north of Comporta. Looking at its position we would definitely be looking to get up close to Porto tomorrow, rather than in no-man's land between Lisbon and Porto as we had previously thought.

We thanked Peter and John very much for the tip, and we bought our new twitcher friends a beer to celebrate. We talked for another hour or so and then we were back in bed by 10pm, tired and excited about the next day's adventures. Thanks for the tip, Peter and John. It really did save us three hours or more and it was a wonderful start to our next day's travel.

Chapter 9

Portugal's 'Golden Gate Bridge' and the Surf Dudes Hotel

Tuesday, 18 September

29°C – clear skies/light cloud

382km travelled today

Breakfast started at 8am and we were there waiting to enter the restaurant area, bikes already loaded and with just our helmets and jackets to collect from the room. We should have opted for no breakfast, as what was on offer was a bit of a let-down – cereal, a couple of cold meats, not forgetting the jam, honey and stale bread rolls.

Maybe we were too early and the fresh supplies had not arrived yet. Even the coffee was poor. Never mind, the hotel in general was great, so maybe this was just an off day. We didn't stay long and we were checked out and on the road by 8.35am, heading for the spit and the Troia ferry over towards Lisbon, just as Peter and John had explained.

It was a little misty this morning and the road was also a little damp. It hadn't rained but you could see everything had a very heavy dew. Our visors were also collecting the wet stuff for the first twenty minutes after we headed off. Heading out of the town on the N-261, we would stay on this road all the way up to the ferry dock.

Looking at the map and the services from the ferry company's website, there were two ferries, one leaving every hour from Sol Troia, the first of the docks we would pass, and the second two miles further on, on the right-hand side at the end of the spit, which also left every hour. We headed for the first ferry port, Sol Troia.

It was a nice ride up, with little to no traffic on the road, especially not travelling back from the ferry port. We rode through the village of Comporta, which was a strange village. It had telegraph posts every 80–100m on both sides of the road, and on the top of every post was a man-made metal flat deck, and on every deck was a stork's nest. There must have been over forty nests, in such a small village. I didn't count the buildings but I would say the storks must have outnumbered the residents by two to one.

We moved on, and on the spit itself there was a lot of sand on either side of the road, which must have meant a full-time job clearing it, as we were riding down the middle of the road to keep out of it. Just before the Sol Troia dock there was what appeared to be a holiday resort, albeit a very quiet one. There were climbing frames and children's play areas, swimming pools, signs for horse riding and lots of cabin accommodation along the roadside, but no people. Maybe the season had finished for this place already. Just to the right was the entrance to the port and we pulled in and paid for our one-way trip at the small desk office. There was no need to get off the bikes as it was a small booth with a window. Only €11 euros each – that's a bargain.

We were the only people at the dock when we pulled up. It had a very small cabin, or bus stop shelter you might call it, and a timetable on the wall. We knew we had twenty minutes to wait for the ferry, as the lady at the ticket office had told us so. We dismounted on the dock and, as other vehicles arrived, we took a few pictures and had good look around. A German family pulled up in their camper van and I asked if they could take a picture of the two of us with our bikes on the dock. They duly obliged and I must say it is great picture.

The sun was shining and the heat was getting up to the mid-twenties now. The ferry docked and we all made our way on to it, parked up and walked up on to the viewing deck. The ferry was not very big, but if fully loaded, I would say you could get twenty-five to thirty cars on it. It was a smooth journey over the estuary and we were enjoying the sunshine as we cruised over to the town of Setubal. From here we would need to take a short stretch of toll road, the A-2 to Almada, which would give us the ride over the 25 de Abril Bridge, a suspension bridge connecting the city of Lisbon, the capital of Portugal, to the municipality of Almada, on the south bank of the river Tagus. If you can visualise the Golden Gate Bridge in San Francisco, this bridge looks like a replica, and it's even painted red just like it.

The autovia was actually a good ride. It was very windy but there was very little traffic on it. Maybe the Portuguese don't like paying the tolls. As we approached the bridge there was a toll gate where we had to pay to ride over it. We agreed to pull over just to the right after the booth area to try to get a picture of the bridge. We tried, but with no luck. As we pulled over, a police car and two police bikes pulled up alongside us; not that we were a target, they just happened to be in the wrong place for us at that specific time.

We moved on and started the ride over the bridge, with its outstanding views of Lisbon. We headed out of Lisbon, staying with the toll road for approximately 40km, as neither of us wanted to take on the local city traffic. So, we picked up the N-257 north-west of Lisbon and we were back on track, heading for dinner at Ericeira. But before we could have dinner we had a great adventure on the hills and roads heading up to the town. My riding skills on the tight corners were getting a little better, and again Dave was nipping off for his speed fix and twisties, as we rode for an hour or so with no traffic.

Approaching our dinner stop we were back in full view of the coastline, and the surf was enormous. To be honest, I don't think I ever imagined Portugal would have such large waves, and they weren't wasted, as all of the beach areas were full of dudes with girls enjoying their sport.

Just before stopping for dinner we pulled into a car park by the beach. We were about 50m above sea level, but we just had to stop for a picture of the surf. The waves must have been 5m high and there were so many people in the water. We weren't the only ones snapping away, as the boardwalk we had stopped on was full of holidaymakers taking pictures of the surf and the beach areas below. Back on the bikes, we headed north again, looking for a café to stop for dinner.

We refilled in a garage 20km later on our right, opposite the coast road, in the village of Casais de São Lourenço, and decided we would have a drink and snack in the café next door. Cheese and ham toasties today, nothing too extreme, and a lovely black Americano with more water to keep us hydrated. Again Dave started to look at the route and where we would stay tonight. We settled on a very nice hotel that was on special offer. The normal price was €89 for a twin room but we got it for €45, including breakfast; another one of Dave's bargain bookings.

Only too soon we were back on the road. We had to go slightly inland for a while now, through some large forested areas. The roads were great, straight with very little traffic. We were passing many areas that looked like they had been burnt in wildfires, as if all the forests had been alight. It was at times very eerie. There were acres of burnt and scorched fields, with places where the remaining tree trunks and shrubbery were charred black. Then we would be back into thick forest and green areas with no trace of any fires.

We were climbing in places through small hills and then back towards the flat lands. We had a great time too, as every so often the road would revert back into a twisted maze of steep corners, rising and descending all too soon back into the straight roads and the forests. Then all of a sudden we entered a village that was full of chimneys, so we stopped and we counted fourteen chimneys that must have been over 30m high.

The road had turned to a bright orange colour, with an orange dust looking like a fine sand polluting the whole area. The reason for this was all too apparent. For almost 3km we rode past scores of terracotta building blocks; not thousands, but what seemed like millions of them, lining the road, five or six pallets high and almost 150–200m back from the road. Then as soon as we had stumbled into the village and its clay block business, it was gone, and we were back on the black stuff.

Not long after this village there was a very familiar smell. I could not quite put my finger on what it was, but it was getting stronger for over a kilometre or so until it all became clear what it was. Coming from Sudbury in Suffolk, there is a huge manufacturing factory, which dominated the industrial areas of Sudbury, working twenty-four hours a day every day of the year. They produce tons and tons of pet food. The downside is that the factory produces a pungent odour around the local area, which was what I could now smell, and I knew it as we rode past the factory in the heart of this forest area here in Portugal. It did put a smile on my face though, as I realised just what the smell was, especially as I hadn't lived in Sudbury for almost ten years now.

We pulled over for our final short stop at Peniche, a seaside municipality, almost an island jutting out from the coastline. It was not the best riding area, as all the roads were cobblestones, but we were here now, so we headed down to the sea front. We had fantastic views both north and south of the headland from the whole coastline. There was a mist being thrown up from the surf below, hitting the beaches and cliff areas of this coastline. Again, if you're ever in the area, it's a lovely walk along the boardwalk, with some fantastic views.

We were only one hour from our hotel of the day and off we set in search of it, crossing the Rio Mondego twice as we entered the town of Figueira da Foz. We could see several fish farms both left and right in the estuary as we drove over the first bridge, with a large area where they were farming salt too, that's if it's called salt farming! We didn't stay to look around the town, as our hotel was in the sticks about 5–6km away. It might only have been a short distance but it took thirty-five minutes to find it. The reason we had trouble finding it was the huge 8ft wall built around the hotel and its grounds, as well as no sign advertising it.

We eventually realised our failings and pushed a small intercom button on a wall that had the smallest hotel sign ever. We were buzzed in and made our way gingerly to reception over more cobblestone roads. We waited ten minutes for the receptionist to check out an elderly couple, then booked into our room. We were booked into a lower-level room in what seemed a brand-new area of the hotel. Within five minutes the receptionist came back and informed us there were works being carried out on this specific room in the morning so he would like to move us to a different room. We both explained that we would be vacating the room by 8am the following day so didn't think changing the room was necessary, so we stayed in the room overnight.

Dave took the opportunity to call Caroline whilst I spent some time writing up the day's events in my journal before taking a shower and heading back into reception and the bar. We had already agreed we would eat at the hotel tonight as we were miles from anywhere and fancied a beer or two as well. So we headed into reception. The bar was an open bar in the reception/restaurant area, which sounds a little strange, but it was well laid out and worked very well.

On the way up we took a quick walk around to look at the strange art hanging from the walls, most of which seemed to show visions of sea views, although I'm no expert and I may be wrong on that too. We also looked over the many surfboards that were on display throughout the hotel. Then it was up the stairs and off for a beer.

We sat outside with a cold Super Bock, this time on draft. It had been a really great day, and we discussed how lucky we both were to be experiencing this journey at such a young age. Little did I know, but in the coming days it would become our journey anthem. Dave would say, "How lucky are we?" and I would reply with, "It is what it is." After a couple of beers we headed into the bar and asked for a table for dinner.

We had by now discovered that the guy who checked us in at reception was called Samuel, who was also the barman and, as we were to find out, the front-of-house and waiter. It reminded me of Mr Ben from my childhood – was there nothing this guy could not do? Well it seemed not. Dave had octopus and I had the chicken stir fry, both very nice, and we followed it with Samuel's recommendation of dark and white chocolate cheesecake, yum-yum … a good finish to a lovely day.

It would be our last comfortable night in a bed for two days, as we had booked ourselves into a campsite some 30km north of Porto for the next two nights. That way we could get our washing done and take a day off before heading back into the northern areas of Spain.

Chapter 10

Two Happy Campers

Wednesday, 19 September

28°C – clear skies

193km travelled today

Breakfast was due to start at 8am but we sat waiting fifty minutes for the staff to set the tables and invite us to sit down, not the best start, but with Samuel not in the hotel this morning, that was obviously the reason why. Never mind, we ate, packed and headed off into the countryside.

If breakfast was a let-down, so was the first hour of the journey. As always, Dave led and I followed, but after thirty minutes of riding out this morning, Dave pulled over and informed me we were going south rather than north, so we had to retrace our route back. Well, even Dave is not perfect. It was not a problem as we knew we were going to have a short day today, especially as the N-109 must have been built by the Romans as it was one long, very straight road.

Finally we were on the right road to our campsite. For the next hour or so we rode through several villages with stork's nests purposely built on the telegraph posts again, but none were anything like the village on the way to the Troia ferry a couple of days back. I was also feeling quite tired today too. We had travelled over 1,450km so far, and with me not being a seasoned biker like Dave, I was feeling it, especially my backside.

We stopped first in a small town called Vagos and parked in the market square, right next to the municipal buildings. There was a fountain to the front of the square, with a staircase leading down to a rural area to the back of the town, where there were many horses grazing and chilling out in the morning sunshine. We just stopped and chilled for thirty minutes, not even looking for a coffee, as it was just a nice place to relax and chat about our first few days of travels. Once again Dave came out with his "How lucky are we …" I'm sure he's not all there sometimes!

Back on the road we were soon on the lookout for a coffee. We were approximately 30km south of Porto when we stopped in the village of Estarreja. We put the bikes on the opposite side of the road in a small car park, in front of the only café in the village. Dave grabbed a table and I headed inside to order two coffees. I asked the guy behind the counter if he spoke English, as I know no Portuguese, but he could not even understand that. The young man with his back to me at the counter turned around and asked if he could help. Within a couple of minutes we had coffee on order as well as some cold sparkling water.

The young man was called Paul, and he had learned a little English at school, and loved the idea of our journey around the coastlines of Spain and Portugal. He was the translator for his three friends, ranging from a young twelve to thirteen-year-old boy to two guys of about my age, late forties, early fifties. They all went over to look at our bikes and they put their thumbs up to show their appreciation. They then wished us good luck as they headed off. We ordered a second coffee and enjoyed the great views of the valley and surrounding area to our left as we sat in the sunshine. It had been a lovely morning and, as always, it's nice to interact with the locals. It was all too soon before we were on our way once again.

We were back on the road within forty minutes and riding on another straight Roman road through to the coast, which then hugged the coastline until we rode through the villages of Brito through to Aldeia, where we filled up once again with fuel before passing through Porto.

We had discussed not going through the city of Porto, as both of us had visited the city over recent years and had also had more than enough of the cobbled roads whilst we had been in Portugal. So, we agreed we would do our best to avoid the city and take a motorway as soon as possible to avoid any chaos.

It was a plan not well executed though, as there was a taxi demonstration on the main autovia we had chosen to avoid Porto, and that threw us straight into the centre of Porto and those cobbled roads along with many other poor motorists. The taxi demonstration was also in full force through the city too, with police directing traffic to avoid the demonstrations, and even though we did not have the intercoms, we really did do well not to lose each other at times. It took us a good hour or more to get through the city and, as we rode up past the main municipality square and through to the main railway station, we both knew where we were, now only a short ride until we hit the main coast road north.

We took a left off the N-13 as we travelled north, but it turned out it was the wrong turning, as we were then straight on to cobbled roads and heading for a small village called Labruge. It was like being back in the dark ages, really small roads, no cars, and expecting to see a horse and cart any minute. We spotted two locals speaking outside a small house and I asked if they spoke English. They said no, but that didn't stop me asking for the camping. They understood what we wanted and told us to ride straight on through the village and we would come to Vila Chã and the campsite. It was another 4km of cobbles and I was sure that much more of these roads and the bikes would start falling to pieces with the vibration, even though I could only travel at 20kph, as I was quite reluctant to go any faster. I guess that's because I was a beginner.

It wasn't too long before we came into the village of Vila Chã, following the signs to the campsite. We parked up, booked into the reception and were shown a small corner of grass right next to a shower block and the washing machines to pitch our tents. I had also packed 20m of rope to make a washing line, so our first job was to be get the washing on, which was not a problem. I had also brought detergent with me but the campsite had this included in the washing machine cycle. Then, whilst the washing was on, we could build our tents.

What a sight that was! I had a new three-man tent from the Spanish outdoor shop Decathlon. It's a great tent and only takes two minutes to pitch. I had used it several times before that summer when my eldest son had visited us in Marbella, so was quite an expert at getting it set up. I can't say the same for Dave though. His tent was a few years old and was a purchase that had been in his attic ever since he bought it. He explained that it was pure coincidence that he had found it when looking for something else for the journey when he initially started getting his gear together for the trip. He had no idea how it went together but it was only fifteen minutes of hard work before he too was ready to become the second half of the happy camping team for the next two days.

Dave was sorting his bike out and I was getting the washing line up ready for the washing that would shortly be finished, and then we could hang it out to dry before it became dark. Once this was done we headed down to the campsite shop to pick up some essentials, so we now had some bread and cheese for breakfast, and toilet roll. We then set out for a walk into the village to get our bearings and stretch our legs. After five days on the bikes both of us needed a walk and a chill out along the coast, leaving the bikes on their own for a few hours.

We were only a five-minute walk from the sea, quite a rocky coastline in this area, with several sandy beaches mixed into the coastline. We headed north on the boardwalk that followed the coast, past a few small beach bars, all of which were closed. It was only mid-September but everything seemed closed already. We walked for about an hour then decided we should head back to get the washing in before going to find a bar and somewhere to eat this evening.

The washing was dry on our return, so we packed it all away and both took a shower. We had been given a free drink voucher when we checked into the campsite earlier so decided to take a drink in the campsite bar first, then see if we could find anything about restaurants in the area from there.

The bar was small but very nice. The lady behind the bar was maybe a little older than me and Dave and she spoke great English. We both had a Super Bock, draft again, and it was a great beer. We also had a free glass of port – well when in Porto, the home of port, you have to try the local drink. Dave plumped for the rosé port and I went for the white port, both of which were served from the fridge, a first for me, as I thought port was always served at room temperature.

We only had the one glass of port, but we did order another beer and asked the lady at the bar were we could eat tonight. She said we should walk into the village to the fishing boats, right on the beach, and carry on south, where we would see two very nice restaurants but she did not know if they would be open. We followed her advice and before too long we were back by the boardwalk, this time heading into the village.

It was like a time gone by when we came to the fishing boats. All ten to twelve of them were pulled up on to the beach, each of them being no more than 12–15ft long, and none were very young either. Just off the beach were a dozen or so huts or sheds all decoratively painted in vibrant colours, with fishing nets hanging around them, as well as lobster pots, buoys of all colours and fish boxes piled up. It looked very industrious but on a very small village scale. It actually turned out that every morning between 9am until they were sold, the local fishermen brought their catches to the beach and sold them to the locals and holidaymakers, on a first-come-first-served basis I would imagine.

We carried on along the boardwalk, having taken a few pictures, then walked past a house that was covered from head to toe in small ceramic tile murals, each depicting either a sea-faring picture or, believe it or not, mythical creatures, ranging from dragons jumping from the sea to flying birds with two heads. It was a house that you just had to stop and look at, and you needed a good fifteen minutes to actually see all the different murals on it.

Still in search of a restaurant, we thought we must be close by now as we were ten-minutes' walk past the fishing boats. Soon, we came to the first of the two restaurants, only to find it was closed. Two minutes further on we found the second restaurant and this too was closed. Great start to the evening, so we headed back into the village.

Directly opposite the ceramic mural house was a village shop. We had seen a few local guys enjoying a beer and coffee in the evening sun earlier so we decided to head back to take a beer and ask inside if there were any other restaurants locally. We entered the shop, wishing the locals a good evening on the way in, but none of them answered; but then if I was sitting with several of my mates in a Suffolk pub and two Portuguese guys walked in and spoke to us in Portuguese, I can't see any of us speaking either.

We sat down inside at one of the three small tables on offer. It was obviously a busy night for the shop, with four guys outside and now two guys inside. The shop looked as though it should have been run by Arkwright and Granville. There was a small cheese section, cooked meat and salamis, as well as fresh meat, bread and cakes. The shelves were stocked with all sorts of tinned food and packets of dry goods too. Next to the entrance door were two large fridges, filled to the hilt with beer and wine, as well as the normal cokes and other soft drinks. It really was an Aladdin's cave.

The shop owner came over after serving a lady who had entered right behind us and had bought some red wine. We asked if he spoke English, which was a no, but he spoke about as much Spanish as I did, which is a little more than nothing. We managed to communicate and ordered two beers. He informed us he was called Manuel, and he ran the shop with his elderly father, who was soon to appear, to start shutting the shop up. On our second beer we asked Manuel if there was a restaurant locally we could walk to. We told him we were camping locally and did not want to drive. No problem. Manuel phoned someone, then told us he had booked a table for thirty minutes' time at the local restaurant. We had time for one more beer and Manuel drew a small map showing us where to find the restaurant.

We paid the bill, €5.40, yes 90 cents a beer, another bargain. We found the restaurant in ten minutes as the directions were really good. It turned out it was right opposite the campsite, about 100m from the entrance. It made the two of us chuckle, but it hadn't been a wasted couple of hours as we had enjoyed the walk, and the fishing boats and ceramic house were a real find, as well as Manuel and his great little bar and village shop.

We walked up the steps to the restaurant and entered what seemed like someone's front room. It was packed. We were seated by a lovely young lady who spoke some good English. She apologised that they were busy and that service would be slow. Suits us fine, we said, and ordered our first beer here. We got the menu on our second beer.

We had worked out that there was a birthday party in, as there were fifteen to twenty locals at several tables that had been moved together, celebrating what we thought was the birthday of one of the ladies. It all looked good fun and we were in no rush. However, the menu was no use to us as it was all in Portuguese, so we had to wait until the waitress came back so she could translate it to us. Fine for Dave, as everything on the menu was fish or from the sea, but I don't eat fish, only meat, and the only thing on the menu for me was a pork steak with chips and a fried egg. So I was fine, I knew what I was having, and Dave went for his favourite once again, octopus. We ordered and took another beer, as we were told that service would be another thirty minutes.

Dinner arrived and we devoured it, as by now it was after 9pm and we had not eaten since breakfast. We were both also a little merry after several beers and no food. The food was good and the bill was only €24 for both meals and four beers each, yet another bargain, and well worth the evening out.

We headed back to the campsite. By now it was very dark with not too much life about. It was our first night camping and I was sure we would sleep like angels tonight. Both tired and half tipsy, we climbed into our tents and it was instant lights out for   me.

Chapter 11

A Busman's Day Off
Drunk in Charge of a Tent!

Thursday, 20 September

28°C – clear skies

181km travelled today

Rising early after a couple of beers the night before and the fact that I was tired, I headed off for a shower. There didn't seem to be anyone about so there was no fight to pick a cubicle. By the time I had showered, shaved and freshened up, Dave was up and setting off for the same routine. I dressed and started making sandwiches from the bread and bits we had bought the day before in the site shop. We had agreed the previous evening that today we would take a ride out to visit some of the lakes in the local countryside and tour around the mountainous area for a few hours.

With our packed lunch made we took another walk along the coastal front, only for an hour, then on our way back stopped for a coffee. We headed into a small coffee shop close to the campsite and I was able to practice some of my Spanish, as the lady owner spoke Spanish too, but no English. Coffee was great and it appeared there was to be a 'women's institute' meeting in the shop as there were several ladies coming in and we seemed to be the topic of conversation, but then again I might well have been wrong.

Heading back to the campsite we got changed into our bike gear by 10.30am, then headed out into the sunshine. It was going to be another sunny day, and Dave's satnav was saying our round trip should be around 130–140km to visit the largest of the lakes on the river Limia in the village of Ponte da Barca.

We headed out from Vila Chã and it was over twenty-five minutes before we would see tarmac. We started on cobbles and Dave's satnav was determined to get us on as many of the local cobbled roads as possible. I was struggling to ride as I was shaking so much and had very little confidence in the handling of the bike on this surface. Not being able to speak to him either was a problem, as he was quite some distance in front and I could see him occasionally stopping for me to catch up.

We managed to weave our way through several very small hamlets, and even on a bike I was praying we met nothing coming the other way, as that could have been quite tricky. Then after about twenty minutes we were making our way through another small hamlet, only to find a refuse lorry filling the road. There was no way we could get around it and we were unsure whether he would back up. One of the workers waved us to pull into a property entrance, not a driveway but a front door entrance just big enough for me to get the bike completely off the road and for Dave's bike to be half off the road, letting the truck squeeze past, as well as the two of us breathing in at the same time.

Finally we hit the black stuff, and not a moment too soon for me. My hands were aching from all the vibration and I was having to remove them from the grips simultaneously every five minutes now just to liven them up. We were just outside the village of Guilhabreu, heading for the town of Muro on the main N-14 going north-east, then picking up the main road at Muro and heading for the town of Trofa, then on towards Vila Nova de Famalicão, crossing the river Via as we rode. It was quite obvious that Dave's satnav had misjudged the distance and time to get to our destination today, even though we had no set time, as it was purely a ride out to chill with no pressure on time, only that we had to be back to eat and have enough time to relax before our coastal journey continued.

By 11.45am we were in the main town of Braga. As we exited the town we could see we were by now starting to climb higher into the mountainous region that we had been heading for, and before long it was all around us. Riding now on the N-101 we were hitting the twisty roads and had views of the valleys all around us as we meandered around this mountainous countryside in a leisurely fashion. Dave was still leading, and at times again today he would shoot off to get his fix of tight bends and corners on this region's roads. I on the other hand was out to use today to recapture the reverse steering techniques and build up some confidence prior to our entering the Pyrenees further on in our journey.

There were several mountain villages that we rode through and it was getting to be real fun as we tackled the steep inclines, with sharp corners on this fantastic road. The surface was also great and I was really enjoying starting to learn how to handle the beast beneath me. We rode into the village of Vado (São Pedro) taking a left turn as we exited on to the very small mountain road the M-532. Once again were on single-file roads and it was a lot of fun.

Dave pulled into a small restaurant that had great views of the river Limia, which was a long way down beneath us. The views were absolutely stunning, with mountains covered in forested areas all around us. The river deep below us away to our left was quite small and narrow in places, then it opened as it meandered through the valley to our right and up into what looked like a large dammed area that really could have been mistaken for a lake and not a river. We took several pictures and headed into the restaurant, then sat outside for a coffee.

I told Dave that my stomach had been rumbling all morning and I didn't feel too great. He too was suffering from the same problem, so we both headed for the toilets one after the other and decided that tonight we would give our restaurant from last night a wide birth tonight. We were fine but just not firing on all cylinders. We didn't eat at this restaurant, we had the packed lunch, but decided we would pick up some water on our way down into the village of Ponte da Barca, which we could see in the distance to our right along the river.

It was only twenty minutes before we were crossing the river Limia, then directly right for what would be our route back towards Barca along the north side river road. Just as we crossed the bridge we could see there were many canoes and pedalos for hire, although not one of them was out today; it was a bit of a ghost town. We headed left over the bridge, around the small roundabout, and there was a small Spar shop. We pulled over and headed in for some water, then off on our travels to find a picnic spot.

We only had to wait five minutes. We were climbing steeply very quickly, and the road was really tricky, some of the best tight corners we had seen on our day so far. We were still in the forests and occasionally getting views of the river below as we climbed higher and higher, then there was to our left, just after a really tight right-hand and left-hand corner, an opening in the foliage where we could see the river below and the views of the valley heading both left and right into the distance. The best thing was that right there in the middle of this opening were two picnic tables and a parking area around them, so that was dinner sorted, and we settled down for a cold water and a cheese and salami sandwich.

We were both feeling a bit rough, and although we weren't in need of running to the toilet every five minutes, we both knew we were nipping the bud so to speak, and very tightly. Dinner was all over quite quickly and we were on the IC-28 riding alongside the river heading west in the direction of Braga.

The roads were giving us both a lot of fun, and I really was enjoying this after the mishap the previous Sunday on my first really tight corner. I was in charge now though, and starting to be at one with my new machine. We crossed the river at Fonte do Monte, where we had to take the autovia A-3 for a short stretch until we could exit and head back to Braga on the N-201. It was becoming a leisurely ride and not too much traffic on the roads either. I was still tired but my backside was holding up well today and that makes all the difference.

We were in and out of Braga within the hour. As we were in the town at a set of lights I asked Dave to miss all the cobbles on the way back and he gave a thumbs up. No such luck though, we were on the cobbles before we knew it and, if I'm honest, it was the only bad part of the whole journey I think. Even my close call when almost crashing and hitting the barriers was not as low as riding on the cobbled roads for such a long time.

Arriving back at the campsite, we were getting showered and changed, as we were once again hot and sweaty after another warm day of riding. We agreed that a sandwich was probably a good idea for our evening meal, as we were starting to feel better but didn't want to risk getting worse – not blaming the restaurant, but it was top of our list. We headed into the site shop once we were clean and changed and bought some lovely large baps, two each, and some fresh ham and cheese to fill them. I had brought my tablet with me to catch up with Vanessa whilst she was on safari and to check my emails too. I headed into the bar and Dave took the shopping back to the tents.

Ordering two beers, as well as a port each, I sat down. The nice lady was behind the bar again and I asked her name, Olivia was the reply. Dave returned shortly after and was moaning that I had bought him beer and a port, but I quickly told him to shut up and stop moaning, jokingly.

The beer was going down really well and so was the port. We started to chat with Olivia and asked where she had learned to speak such good English. It turned out that her father was a diplomat back in the 60s when she was very young. He was then posted overseas with the family to what used to be the colonial country of Rhodesia. It was at this time that she was in an English school for several years, but when unrest started in the early 70s her father and family moved back to Portugal. It was a lovely story to hear and she had some lovely memories of her time there with her family.

As we were discussing Olivia's English, as well as trying to stop Dave from continuing to wind me up about the port and beer he was forcing himself to drink, an English couple entered the bar and sat at the table next to us. We all introduced ourselves, and our new friends were Helen from Hastings and

Gareth from Lancashire, who were here on a costal walking holiday. Gareth had visited several times before and really loved the region. It appeared that our new friends were not too long acquainted, as they were very touchy feely and on one or two occasions I did think they needed to get a room! Or maybe a tent …

They left before too long as they had a table booked at the restaurant we had eaten in the night before. Neither me nor Dave mentioned our stomach problems of today and we wished them good luck and a nice holiday. The time must have been close to 8pm, as I can remember the reservation Helen and Gareth had was at that time, and by now we were both feeling very merry.

We spent the rest of the evening drinking. I would like to say I remember in full, but to be honest I can't, as both Dave and I were now three sheets west and all I remember is trying to walk back to our tents after leaving the bar sometime after 10pm. The only reason I remember that it was 10ish is a faint memory of me and Dave trying to push each other over on the walk back, and one of us mentioning the fact that we had not eaten and it was now 10pm in the evening.

We calmed down a little, and the next and final memory I have of the evening is opening my tent, or trying to. Each time

I leant down to raise the zip to open the door I was stumbling forward and then quickly standing up to prevent myself from falling over. This then sent me scurrying backwards in the opposite direction. I was in a real mess, but at least I hadn't fallen over. That distinction was to come to Dave, who was also having problems with the zip on his tent, the difference being he couldn't stand up quickly enough, and all of a sudden there was a huge crash bang wallop and Dave was laughing his head off and lying all over his two-man tent. I immediately went into hysterics, and I was in such a mess, but all I can remember is asking Dave if he was going to be spending the night on his tent or actually in it.

The rest of the night I remember nothing, not even getting into my tent. I did, however, wake up with a very sore head and a mouth like a dog's backside at 7.45am. Dave was inside his broken tent. It was apparent that he had broken one of the main supports and the tent was looking very poorly. We spent the next hour reminiscing about the night before and winding each other up. Like two small infants, but we had had a good night and no harm done, albeit a little to Dave's self-esteem, and I had bragging rights for an hour or two.

Chapter 11

Back to España and a Night Out with a Turkish Glaswegian as Our Host

Friday, 21 September

24°C – clear skies, light cloud

214km travelled today

Packing up really was a struggle this morning, as we both had heads that were fit for nothing. We missed our evening meal last night due to alcohol overload, and somehow there was nothing left to eat anyway. It looked as if Dave had the munchies all night to me. We slowly showered and started packing our cases and taking the tents down. Neither of us were in a hurry and I'm sure Dave felt just the same as I did – I could at any time have just gone straight to the closest hotel to sleep the hangover off.

By 10.30am we had managed to get shipshape and our journey was about to resume as we rode out of the campsite. It was only a ten-minute ride on the cobbles back to the N-13 coast road north, but that ten minutes lasted a lifetime for me as my stomach was going over and over. I even had to stop to make sure my helmet was fully open just in case I had the urge to throw out the last of last night's port and beer.

We both made it to the main road without mishap and in one piece. If I'm honest, looking back, I know we had taken our time in the morning packing up but we really should not have been on the bikes. We slowly headed north and it was only on occasion that we could see the actual coast, as the road was a kilometre or so away from the sea.

We rode over the river Ave estuary at Azurara, carrying on north through several hamlets and costal harbour villages. The largest of the towns on our ride north was the town of Fão to the south of the river Cávado estuary, then we passed over an old iron bridge that spanned a large island in the middle of the next estuary, leading to the town of Esposende on the north side. The estuary was really wide, and although the towns were scattered to the immediate north and south of each bank of the river, there was not too much else around, and the mountains had disappeared into the far distance, the surrounding area looking more of a flat marsh land.

Time was moving on, especially as we had left late today, and we stopped on the Portuguese border with Spain at

Caminha. We pulled over at a small ferry terminal and parked the bikes up outside the small café in the car park. There were two lovely ladies inside and we were both starving. There was nothing but baguettes on offer but they were freshly made and we could choose our filling. We both went for the standard ham and cheese, plus a large black coffee each and water to try to rehydrate us both.

We discussed whether we should take the ferry over the estuary of the river Minho, but we both felt that the sea might be one step too far for our delicate situations. So we sat and ate our baguettes, drunk our coffee and started to recover as we watched the small ferry arrive and unload its cargo of three cars and one push bike. There was one car waiting to board and also a small bus full of Chinese or Japanese holidaymakers.

But we would ride on and take the first bridge over the river, then head into Spain in the direction of Vigo, thus skirting around the largest estuary we would see that day and the river Vigo. I was starting to enjoy the ride now after dinner, and the weather was not as hot as it had been previously. The roads were in great condition, and with dinner sitting well, the journey was an enjoyment again.

The plan was to find a café in an hour or so and have a break, then find where we could bed down for the night. We skirted around Vigo and were on the estuary road going north, through the small village of Redondela on the N-550, when Dave pulled over. We had a quick chat and decided to go inland for a while and take on a short stretch of mountain roads that Dave had seen on the satnav. I was fine with that and said we could have a coffee en route.

So off we headed, and before too long we were on some really narrow mountain roads, with the odd house and small farm scattered along the route. We soon rode into Saramagoso, a small village with approximately forty properties, and a café in the centre. It was the largest village we had seen in twenty minutes, so a good place to pull over. I headed over to the café whilst Dave sorted his life out on the bike.

I ordered coffee and water and watched the locals playing cards and drinking their coffee and brandies. The man behind the counter was a man of very few words, and once he had served me he walked round to my side of the counter and laid down for a nap on a sofa. Dave came in and we looked at our choices for a hotel this evening. We decided on a town further north called Vilagarcia de Arousa, which didn't look much on a map, but the hotel had a cheap room, so we booked it without a breakfast.

By the time we had finished the coffees all the locals had left, apart from the three playing cards. I thought we had been the topic of their conversation since we arrived; sometimes you can just sense what is being said, even if you can't speak much of the language. As we walked out I wished everyone a good day in Spanish as well as in English and we were also wished a safe journey by one of the locals in English too. It's nice when that happens.

We mounted up and had about an hour and a half to the hotel at a moderate pace. We weaved our way back to the main road, the N-550, which would take us north before we would then head west into the town of Vilagarcia de Arousa. It was a lovely finish to the day's riding, with some quite challenging inclines and narrow roads on the way, but before too long we were at the hotel and parking in its car park at the rear, next to the outside swimming pool that was covered with a very large conservatory building.

Checking in, we had to move the bikes, as the manager wanted us to park on the opposite side of the car park. I don't know why, but we moved them anyway. The room was great and the shower hot. We settled in for an hour's snooze to catch up on the night before, then showered and headed into town for a meal.

We were about a kilometre outside the main town area and there were many places to eat on the Google Maps page we were looking at. We chose to walk alongside the sea from the hotel as there was a lovely paved promenade, and twenty minutes later we were in the town and it was very busy. We mooched about for around thirty minutes and just had a good time understanding what was going on around us.

We stopped first at a large outside bar/restaurant but they were only serving drinks and no food at that time, so we didn't stay, and we wandered off. The next place we came to was packed. Every table was taken, the locals were drinking, and everyone had Spanish omelette too, so we headed inside for some of it ourselves.

I asked the waitress if she spoke any English but she just looked with a blank expression and walked away. A minute later a young guy from behind the counter came over and asked in English if he could help us. We ordered two draft beers and asked about a menu. He told us we could only get tortilla (Spanish omelette), so we asked for two of them.

The beers came, along with two small slices of the tortilla and a small slice of chocolate cake each. We were both a little confused as to why we only had a couple of small pieces of tortilla. I managed to get the attention of the guy behind the counter and asked for some more tortilla, which came over, and again with a small piece of cake. At this rate we would be there all night to get a decent meal, so we decided to cut loose and find another place to eat. It wasn't until the bill came and it was only €2.40 that we realised that the tortilla was free when buying a drink, and I had asked for a second portion, which again they had not charged us for. It was something that was going to become the norm in most places over the rest of the journey.

Heading out we both felt as if we had taken advantage of the last restaurant. We looked around again and almost all restaurants were opening at 8.30pm for food. The time was now just before 8pm and we were ravenous. We had seen a bakery with loads of pizza for sale as we first entered the town, and it was doing a roaring trade, so decided we would head back in that direction and, if we had not found anywhere to eat by then, we would grab a pizza.

Just before the pizza bakery there was a kebab restaurant just opening for the evening. Dave and me looked at each other and we had the same thought – after a skin full yesterday, what else would suit our stomachs better than a nice greasy kebab and chips. We asked the young guy if he was open and he said not yet but we could come inside for a drink while he opened up. So we went in, sat down, and were given a menu.

It turned out the young guy was the owner's son. The owner, Hamid, came over and introduced himself. He was a really interesting guy and it transpired he was of Turkish descent but from Iran. He had lived for four years in London and had a kebab takeaway there with his brother. He then moved to Glasgow, and it was the Glaswegian accent we could hear dominating his English. Mind you, it was a fun accent to hear from a Turkish-Iranian who lives and works in Spain. He explained that he had been in Spain now for over fifteen years and his restaurant was very popular, but not at such an early time. The town would not get lively until 11pm to midnight, and he closed at 3am in the morning, so he must have some very good late-night trade.

We both ordered lamb kebab with lots of meat and salad, and both with chips. I was on the water and Dave was on the Fanta. We talked away with our new-found friend until dinner was served. Dinner did not disappoint. The greasy lamb was great, with a whole plate full of salad and a side plate of chips. We did all we could to eat everything given to us but alas we could not. We did, however, both have another drink afterwards and stayed for over an hour chatting with Hamid, finishing off with a coffee before asking for the bill.

The best was to come. We had chosen the lamb meal deal, and at €6 your drinks were included. The only extra charge we had was a plate of chips each, so we had a total bill for the two of us of under €15, what a bargain. If you're ever in Vilagarcia de Arousa, and in need of a great restaurant, head for Ali Baba's Kebab shop, you won't be disappointed.

We walked back along the promenade. It was 9.30ish by now, and as we walked back to the hotel it seemed the whole town was now going out in the opposite direction into town. We must be getting old. In the shallows we could see several guys harvesting something from the sea into rowing boats that they were pulling along with them. On closer investigation we decided it was seaweed they were harvesting. The sun was now setting and the sea was very flat, with little to no wave movement. It was a very pretty end to what had started out a challenging day earlier, as well as being a great night with our new friend Hamid and his son.

Chapter 12

Journey to the Cathedral

Saturday, 22 September

30°C – clear skies, mist and fog in the morning

366km travelled today

We awoke to a first on this trip, thick fog and a really heavy dew everywhere. We weren't staying for breakfast so it was a quick exit this morning as we said goodbye to another lovely hotel. The plan was to head north towards Noia and the Bogelleira estuary for coffee and breakfast.

I can't say it was slow going, as there was no traffic on the road and we had no set destination for the day, but the conditions did keep us to a slow ride until we stopped in Noia for breakfast and our first stop of the day. Parking on the main road in the town, we were next to a small but nice paved square with several coffee shops, all of which were open, but when we arrived at 10.30am there were not too many people about.

It was one of those lovely stops. We sat down and a young lady came over to take our order. My Spanish was working well this morning and the coffee was on order, as well as the breakfast menu card, with not one query from the girl about what it was I was asking for. I think Dave was just as impressed as I was today.

Coffee came and I asked if there were any pastries, as they were not on the menu card. She told us there were only croissants, so we ordered one each. They were on the table within a minute or two, and what a croissant it was, full of warm chocolate and the size of a small loaf. We were both impressed and it was a really good start to the day, as the coffee was also great, as I've found nearly always to be the case in Spain.

We both popped into the toilet, and the café was like an American diner inside, with rows of booths and all sorts of American memorabilia, ranging from Elvis mirrors on the walls to bootlegging pictures of the 1930s, and the odd baseball picture too. Mickey Mouse took centre place on the wall behind the bar and it really was a nice quaint place, and one I will always remember for the huge breakfast croissants. Maybe I should have had two!

The fog was slowly lifting as we rode out of town at 11am, heading north on the AC-550 and due to cross the next estuary at Punta Seilán, over a very long bridge with some awesome views both left and right. Dave pulled up at the side of the road as there was still no traffic and we both took a few pictures. It was an eerie feeling, with small mountains in the distance, the estuary surrounding us on both sides of the bridge, and the mist still lifting, giving some lovely views, with a real early morning feel to the landscape and what it had to offer. If I'm honest, it looked rather surreal.

We set off once again, and within two minutes we were once again parked at the side of the road on yet another bridge, taking pictures of this amazing morning's scenery. My most prominent memory of that morning is the two bridges and the mist rising, with the forests leading down to the water's edge and the mountains only visible in places as the mist was still holding on to them prior to the sun warming up sufficiently to take them away.

Heading out of Noia, we decided not to turn back to collect the coast road straight way as this would have put another 200km on our journey, but to head in a north-west direction to pick up the coast at A Ponte do Porto. This journey was to take the coast road, but not at any cost. Let's face it, it was our journey to tour these two countries. We had a lovely ride up to Dumbria, passing through several small villages as we rode through this very hilly region. The roads were in great condition, and by noon the sun was beaming down on us once again just to make sure we didn't have the whole day in the fog.

Taking the AC-552 out of Dumbria, we headed north to the village of Berdoias, where we would pick up the CP-9202 to our left that would take us all the way to A Ponte do Porto. The roads were giving us a lot of fun, and for over an hour on our journey there we didn't see a single soul. If only we'd known that before, I think I might have been as adventurous as Dave as he kept speeding off to enjoy himself. Don't get me wrong, I was loving the day just as much as Dave, but I did have in the back of my mind that I needed to be pushing myself with the cornering and the manoeuvring of the bike. I was a week into my motorcycling career now and impatience was starting to take over.

It was a brief ride through the town and over the next estuary at A Ponte do Porto. It was a brief sight of the sea now before our last section of the day, inland before heading for the main coastline, which we would follow for the afternoon until we arrived at Laxe. This was to be the most westerly point of the journey in Spain and the start of a really great afternoon, but first we decided to head into the town and park up by the seafront to have a coffee.

Riding into the port town was again one of those steep descents. There was not too much going on and we parked the bikes next to a sand dune area with a coffee shop on one side of us and a restaurant on the other. We ordered coffee and wondered where the sea was. As I waited at the table for coffee, Dave took a walk over the sand dunes and informed me we were only 50m from the sea and a huge cove that, for whatever reason, had been hidden from us on our ride down into the town. It was too hot for me now to walk over the sand dunes so I took Dave's word for it.

We drank our coffees, which had arrived with a piece of chocolate cake as a free tapas – how I love this country. We then paid up and headed out to a very small coast road out of town, which gave us some great views of the town and the cove we had just left, as well as a small port to the far end of the town.

We were now on what can only be described as C-roads, and these hugged very steep cliff edges to our left and a very hilly and mountainous region to the right of us inland. I lost count of the number of inlets and coves we pulled over to take pictures of. The sea was a light turquoise throughout the whole afternoon, and when we passed coves with sandy beaches, the sea really could have been mistaken for anywhere in the Caribbean.

Within the hour we pulled in to refuel just south of A Coruña, then headed north-east. We were back inland for a short period before skirting around Sada and on to the small town of Ferrol. We now took the AC-566 north, where the surrounding region was thick with forests. We were still being wowed by the wonderful coastal views every so often, as well as having lots of fun on the twisty roads around this north-west corner of the coast.

By 2.30pm we were getting peckish, so Dave pulled into a lovely little restaurant that was in the middle of nowhere. It couldn't be too bad though, as the car park was heaving. We sat outside at the only free table available, waiting for service, but after ten minutes it didn't seem like we were going to get any, so I popped inside to order. As we were both hungry by now, we were on the lookout for food as well as a drink.

The place was clean but it was a little run down inside. The tables looked like they had been in the place since the 50s, as did the chairs come to think of it. It was very busy inside and, not for the first time, I could feel many eyes on me as I stood waiting to be served. There were stuffed wild boar heads hanging on the walls, ranging from young to old, and quite large. Surprisingly there were no deer or stag trophies, only around a dozen wild boar.

It was me next, and the guy asked what I would like. Once again my Spanish was going well, coffee was ordered, as well as two sparkling waters, but there was no food. Don't ask me why, maybe it was too late, being after 2.30pm. He did explain but my Spanish really is not that good. Then he informed me I could get some local tapas dishes shortly, and he would bring the coffees etc. out to us.

I set to explaining what I thought was happening to Dave, and the guy soon arrived with coffees, water and some lovely fresh cake. No idea where that came from, although we weren't complaining. He said tapas would be ten minutes. As always, the coffee was lovely and so was the cake. We caught sight of the guy shortly after and ordered two more coffees, which arrived with what was to be one of the strangest dishes we would see on our journey.

The guy laid down the coffees and explained that here in Northern Cataluña the wild boar is the best meat to be found. (Well that's what I think he was telling us. Like I said, my Spanish is not great). One of the local dishes is a small donut with a slice of port belly on top, skewered together with a small wooden party stick. There were two plates of them, each with six portions on the plate.

The guy left us whilst me and Dave both looked at each other wondering whether this guy was having us on or whether it was true what he had told us. It didn't matter too much though, as Dave said, we could eat them with the pork belly as the main course, followed by the donuts, or just dive in, as they would all end up in the same place. I have to admit I couldn't argue with him, so we took the guy at his word and ate the strange tapas pork belly donuts, and they were really delicious.

The guy came back out ten minutes later with some more cake and asked whether we had enjoyed the tapas. Then he spoke to the people at the two tables next to us, which were full of more local 'women's institute', and they were all laughing about whatever he had told them. I told Dave that my guess was that he said to them, "These bloody stupid English will eat anything we give them if we tell them it's our tradition." Dave agreed with me, but what the hell, we didn't care, it really was nice.

Time was moving on now and it was well past 3pm. Dave had found us a hotel called the Hotel Playa de las Catedrales. We were about 70km away, but with the roads we were on it was at least a two to two-and-a-half-hour ride. The afternoon didn't disappoint either, the stunning coastal scenery carried on, with some wonderful hidden beaches and coves, followed by steep cliffs and the most beautiful colour sea you could have wished for.

We stayed with the small roads all afternoon. I really did feel that I was in total charge of the bike today and really enjoying the cornering, especially when they were to a right-hand turn, with the odd steep incline on the exit. It was giving me a buzz that made me feel great. As with most things that are enjoyable, time seems to disappear very quickly, and before we knew it the time was closer to 6pm and we were now looking to find the hotel as we rode down the main coast road, the N-634. We missed the turning first time around and had to make a U-turn to get on the road down to the beach and the hotel.

The hotel was quite a large place and quite modern. It had a large car park that was almost empty as we arrived. We parked up, then headed inside to check in. The young man on reception was really nice and very helpful, also courteous, as he asked us to wait for a moment whist he answered the phone. We were checked in, then the guy asked if we would like to have our free entrance ticket to the Catedrales now or in the morning. We had no idea what he was talking about, but he then explained that the hotel is named after the short stretch of coast it sits on, the Playa de las Catedrales, which translates to beach of the cathedrals.

This coastal stretch of sand is about a kilometre long, yet packed with a most unusual series of geological formations. This beach alone proves that Mother Nature had a fondness for flying buttresses before any human engineer patted himself on the back for coming up with the now-iconic architectural feature. The most stunning of these has been named La Catedral (the cathedral) and can be visited only at low tide twice a day. It was low tide as we were checking in so he advised that we take a walk to see it tonight before nightfall and visit early, between 8am and 10am in the morning.

Our room was nice, clean and had a view from two storeys up to the bikes below. I sat and chilled and made my journal notes as Dave showered. I followed shortly after, as we were both hungry, but first, as we had been on the road a week, Dave suggested we give a full once over to both bikes. Not a problem for me, as I have no idea what needs to be carried out, but down we went and I learned for the first time how to oil my chain and check the suspension on the bike. We tested all the lights etc., as well as the oil, once Dave had found where my oil level indicator was. Then it was back upstairs for another quick wash before setting off to find food. We asked the young guy on reception, who recommended the beachfront restaurant only ten minutes' walk away, which he said had a nice bar and great food.

We walked down to the place, which was very busy. The car park in the hotel was almost full by now, and arriving at the restaurant we didn't have too many tables to choose from, and there must have been over forty tables set outside, as well as those inside. Our waitress was very sweet, but she spoke no English, so once again I was the gringo in charge. We ordered two large beers and asked for the menu. Everything once again was in Spanish only; I don't think there are too many Brits visiting this area. Dave went for the largest sea bass I've ever seen and I had a pork loin with fried eggs and chips. The waitress placed her fingers to her mouth and made that Italian gesture of approval on the port loin.

It seems we tend to rate each day on the roads we ride, the views we see, the hotel where we sleep, and finally the food we eat. This was to be a perfect ten on my scorecard as the food was outstanding. The quantity was way too much, even for a lump like me at sixteen stone plus, so Dave helped me polish it off. We ordered another beer and just sat discussing the day's ride, as it had been another great day on the road.

We were people watching now, and the oldest hippie in town had just pulled up opposite the restaurant, then went for a walk along the beach with his dog. There were couples of all ages just enjoying the beach and the whole area. Maybe I will return one day with Vanessa, as I'm sure she too would like the whole region.

It was dusky by now and we were both stuffed, so we finished our beer and paid the bill. Oh, and the port loin I had was only €12, absolute bargain of the week. If you're ever in the area, I fully recommend it. You can't miss the restaurant as it's the only one at the end of the road past the hotel, right on the small coast road.

We took a short walk up and along the coast road path and on to the boardwalk, as most other people seemed to be doing. We were looking for the gothic coastline and it didn't disappoint. It reminded me of the time when Vanessa and I had driven along the Great Ocean Road in Australia and stopped at each of the Twelve Apostles. That is the kind of scenery you're in for when visiting this beach, quite breathtaking. We took a few pictures and discussed our upcoming morning. Although we would have liked to visit the beach below in the morning, especially having the ticket entrance too, we thought we would be too late leaving the hotel at about 11am after returning from the walk. With that in mind we agreed we would head off without visiting it and leave Las Catedrales on the to-do list for the future.

Chapter 13

Heading Inland in the Mist

Sunday, 23 September

28°C – heavy cloud and mist, sunshine late afternoon

397km travelled today

We were both up early this morning. Breakfast was an option but we were still both full from the night before. Leaving without breakfast we decided we would head out, as the weather was a very thick and heavy sea mist. Good job we didn't wait to visit the La Catedral today as we would never have seen it with this weather.

Riding out, we were going to be hugging the coast all morning, but we rarely saw the coast due to the mist. In places we could only see 50m in front of us. Traffic was very light, hence we made a good 70km in the first hour and a half as we travelled along the main N-634 in search of a breakfast stop.

After some of the arid dry landscapes we had travelled through over the first seven or eight days we were now in a very lush green region, with small hills and mountains, and thick forests covering most of region. As we rode on, to our right and left we could just make out the coast in the heavy mist, with its steep cliffs and green meadows leading towards them.

By 10am we were stopping at a small hamlet called Villapedre. When I say hamlet, the café was the first building on our left as we parked up on our side of the road. There were four other buildings all on the same side as the café. Not the biggest place to stop, but there were over ten cars parked along the road and it did look half full as we entered. There was nowhere to sit inside the place, so we headed to the patio area outside, to the side of the building, which was enclosed with what seemed like a huge tent covering the tables. It also had a couple of gas heaters in it to warm the place up, not that we were overly cold, but with no sunshine and an outside temperature this morning of 12°C, we weren't exactly warm either.

We both decluttered our jackets and helmets etc., and headed into the café, where we ordered two coffees. We could see that we were in for a real treat today for breakfast. There were two ladies behind the bar, one serving customers and the other was the chef. We were like two little schoolboys as our faces lit up, because we could see the chef making egg and bacon rolls for five local guys sitting inside the place. At exactly the same time we asked each other, one or two? We both laughed and ordered four egg and bacon rolls. The lady said it would be twenty minutes, so we ordered another coffee to come with them when they were ready.

This gave us time to take a look at our route for the day in more detail. We decided to keep away from the motorways at all costs, to try to see as much of the coast as possible, that is if the mist ever rose. We had another 180km plus to do before we hit any real major roads, half of which would be along the main coast road before heading inland to ride around Gijón, and not through it. Back on to the N-632 coast road once past Gijon, it would only be an hour or so until we were then climbing into the Parque Nacional de los Picos de Europa, heading now inland to what would be the start of the foothills of the Pyrenees.

The breakfast rolls were great, so was the coffee that washed them down. It's strange that when you're not with your wives and partners, when given the healthy option when eating, or the low cholesterol option for breakfast, you never seem to take the healthiest one. It was getting on for forty-five minutes that we had been at the café so it was time to leave.

The rolls worked out €1.80 each and the coffees were €1.00 each. Where else can you get a breakfast like that for €5.20 – yet another of those holiday bargains.

Dave was back in front and, as always with no intercom, I was following. We were staying with the N-634 and we were very tight at times to the coast and cliff edges too. The mist was slightly improved but it was keeping our speed down to 80kph. The road through was deserted, and what fun I had this morning, with full trust in the bike as well as my ability as a week-old motorcyclist. I would say I was pushing it hard, as it really felt like it at times. Dave even waved me through for a while, as I think he wanted to see just how I was coping with the roads, as well as make a judgment on my progress on my two-wheeled beast.

Regardless of who was leading, I was having a really great day. If you're not a rider, I can only explain that today was a time for me riding the bike when I actually felt like I was a part of the machine and not just riding it. It's a strange statement I know, but a true one, nevertheless.

It was getting on now for 12.30pm and we had covered another 80km since our restart. It had been endless twists and turns as well as steep cliffs to our left most of that time. We entered the town of Soto del Barco, parking just off the main roundabout as we came into the town at an open café. The waitress came out and we ordered coffee. It was, though, a frightening sight. I'm no waif I must admit, but she was larger than me at sixteen stone and clad in bright-red leopard print skin-tight leggings and a white T-shirt that looked three sizes too small. On the front of the T-shirt were printed two hand prints. I will leave it to your imagination where the hand prints were. Like I said, frightening.

She made good coffee though, and as per usual in the northern regions of Spain, we had a free tapas with the coffee, this time a lovely chocolate cake each, a bit like a muffin, only a little smaller. We only had the one coffee as Dave looked up our options for a hotel for tonight. We settled on the hotel that Dave had stayed in two weeks prior, after landing at Santander on his first day in Spain. It was about another three hours away and would give us a great ride through the foothills and national park this afternoon to get there. Whilst looking up the hotel I worked out that the route we had taken on the coast road since breakfast had been approximately 80km, but if we had taken the motorway to Soto del Barco it would have been 21km to get where we were for coffee. It just goes to show how twisty the roads were that morning.

It was a quick stop and we were on the road again by 1pm, this time heading slightly inland to miss the coastal town of Gijón. We were now starting to pick up altitude too as we headed away from the coast. In places we were climbing on single-file roads as Dave cut his way overland and through the national park areas en route to Liérganes, the destination for our hotel tonight.

The mist finally started to lift around 2pm. There was a much-appreciated rise in the temperature too, and finally I could feel the warmth on my back. The roads were great, and we were now seeing more forestry and less and less of the coastline as we rose through this region, where we were given only the occasional opening to see the sea in the distance.

We entered the town of Arriondas, our last stop for the day, where we refuelled in the small town and decided to take a coffee and some liquids, as the sun had turned up at last. We parked in the small town centre, on a square full of cars and coffee shops. We sat down at the back of the café on a patio area, had a coffee and watched the world go by right next to the river that ran beneath us. There were children everywhere in their canoes, as well as some rowing boats with couples rowing along in the sunshine. We were discussing the traffic today and between us we could only count seven cars that we had seen on the roads since leaving in the morning, with the exception of the stops we had made. We really were travelling alone.

We were once again off, tanks full and in search now of our hotel. This was to be the very best part of the day, with the single-file roads meandering through the region and climbing though several small valleys, and stopping several times for the odd picture of the views on offer. There were no villages, only the odd hamlet or single property scattered along the route.

It was coming to an end for the day and it was just before 4.30pm when we pulled up at the hotel, where we parked the bikes off-road directly in front of the hotel entrance. We checked into the hotel, or I should say Dave did, while I was being nosey in the reception area, just looking at an old table that was standing there. It was a very strange thing; a very solid construction, with legs that must have been six inches square, and the top of the table was split into two sections that sat alongside each other, which were also approximately six inches thick and each piece a foot wide.

What really intrigued me was the carving on the top of the table, which was almost as if the table had small scales carved into the surface. In the end I had to ask the receptionist what it was, or what it was used for. She smiled and told me that I was not the first person to ask this question. The table was thought to be over three hundred years old, and it was used as a wheat threshing table. The wheat would be cut at the bottom of its stem and then would be threshed on the table to get the wheat corns off the stems and husk. Simple when you know what it is.

The room was very comfortable and we both chilled for a couple of hours, then showered and tidied out our travel cases. Vanessa had sent through some lovely pictures and small videos from her safari holiday and we also managed to have a brief chat on WhatsApp before she lost connection at her end. I once again brought my journal up to date, and at about 7pm we headed out for a walk and to find some dinner.

There is a lovely small river running through the town and two bridges crossing it. It seemed that everyone was out tonight, as most Spanish do on Sundays, all dressed in their Sunday best and just strutting their stuff along the river. We decided on a nice-looking hotel restaurant that Dave recommended from his previous stay. We went in, sat down and asked for two beers and a menu but were told that the kitchen didn't open until 8.30pm on a Sunday. As you can imagine that was no problem to me and Fat Man. That just meant we would have to have a few beers before we ate.

The young waiter brought the beers over and we had a chat with him, as he spoke very good English. He was really interested in our journey and just how far we would be riding over the three weeks, and he too wished he had the time and finances to do such a great journey. We had a couple more beers and at about 8pm the waiter came over and gave us a wink and the menu. The chef was in and we could order as soon as we liked.

It was more pork tonight, but this time it was a house special, pork belly, fried eggs and chips, and the young waiter said we would have two chorizo sausages that the chef makes himself. Very Spanish, but never underestimate the pork belly in Spain as they are masters of cooking this great cut, and the chorizo were absolutely delicious.

Food was on the table within fifteen minutes, and didn't take much longer than that to leave the table too. It was very tasty, and although our new friend the waiter did try to talk us into a slice of apple pie, we just couldn't fit it in. Instead, we ordered a coffee and then asked for the bill. Once again our bill was unbelievable. We were charged only for two beers each, even though we had drunk four, the food was only €7.50 each, and with no coffee charged either. Dave queried it with the waiter but he was adamant it was correct and wished us a very safe journey. So, with a total bill of under €20 euro we left €40 on the table and thanked the waiter for his service.

It was a short walk back to the hotel, and there were just as many people walking through the town and along the river as earlier. We didn't stop in the hotel bar for a beer. It was only 9.45pm but we were both tired and tomorrow was another big day, as every day was on this journey. There was a light drizzle in the air but hopefully tomorrow would be dry. Let's face it, the only rain we had seen so far was on our very first day, way back down near Tarifa, and we were lucky that day that we made it to the hotel when we did. Tomorrow we were heading north-east and up towards the Pyrenees. The hype Dave had given that region was going to be something that needed to be lived up to. Bring it on ...

Chapter 14

Blinded by Rain and Mist but no Longer a Slowcoach

Monday, 24 September

18°C – heavy rain and mist until late afternoon

331km travelled today

There was no need for an early start today, as neither of us wanted to vacate the hotel because it was pouring with rain. We took breakfast at 9am, which was a nice buffet, but in all honesty nothing to write home about and definitely nothing like the egg and bacon rolls from yesterday.

We pootled about trying to convince ourselves the rain was going to stop, but we did have to get moving though. Dave said we wouldn't get too wet, and it was 10am by the time we were leaving, with the rain due to stop within the hour. How bloody wrong was he?

We set off, and it was raining just as Peter Kay would say, the wet stuff, the rain that goes right through you. There was also a really thick mist as we were heading on the back roads for the most of the morning. We did have the choice of motorway but if we were going to get wet, we thought we might as well be enjoying the ride as we rode on.

The roads were ... well, let's just say they weren't A-roads, B-roads or even-C roads. These were mountain roads, extremely narrow, and tight corners with steep inclines and steeper descents. For the first hour who cared about the rain? We started off dry and it took the first hour for both of us to start to feel the damp seeping into our skin. But during that hour we were having the time of our lives. I was doing all I could at 40–55kph just to keep Dave in my sights, the mist was so thick, and the higher we got it became really thick cloud and really wet too. At times we were down to 30kph as we just had no idea where the road was. The fun was in full force though. These roads were so narrow in places that even a car would struggle to keep on the black stuff. We didn't see another vehicle all morning. It must have been the mad Englishman's morning today, and everyone else had either stayed in bed or decided to work from home.

Dave pulled over just after 11am to ask if I was getting wet. Stupid bloody question! I was, and it gave me great joy to know that Dave was also wet and he was the one with a brand-new all-weather suit. That lifted my damp morale and made me enjoy the rain for the rest of the morning, knowing he was just as uncomfortable as me. How little things please us poor old and miserable men!

We agreed to carry on and find a coffee shop where we could try to warm up a bit. The closest town was Arredondo, only 7km away, but that was to be another twenty-five minutes by the time we had taken on yet another very steep incline, with the sharpest left-hand and right-hand corners that I had had to navigate so far. The left-hander going in was almost a 180-degree turn, with a very sharp and steep incline as I turned into it. Then it was a short 70m straight with what must have been a 230-degree right-hander and still gaining altitude very quickly as I went around. The buzz for me as a novice was awesome. All I kept telling myself, though, was what Dave had told me the night before, that when you're on a tight corner and it's a steep rise, do not stall the bike, as it was a certainty I would drop it and it would be a two-man job to get it back up. No pressure there then for me the beginner. I was enjoying the ride though. The roads, although hard to master for me, were giving lots of fun, and this together with the concentration in the rain and thick cloud was giving a real adrenaline rush.

We rode down into the small town of Arredondo and pulled up outside a row of three cafés, where we sat down at the first one, The Casanova. We were both feeling a little deflated now we had stopped and Dave was looking at where to stay tonight. Our ideal destination was Pamplona, but the route we had in mind earlier in the morning was all small roads and would take all day, with over 380km to travel. Our expected arrival would be after 5pm in the afternoon.

We ordered coffee and they came with the now normal helping of chocolate tapas cake. Yes it was free, as was deemed the norm now. We decided to give it another hour in the rain, then if it had not stopped we would reassess our situation and maybe take the motorway to Pamplona and possibly do some washing etc., as we could be there by 2pm if we changed to this option.

With a new plan now hatched we set off to give the weather the benefit of the doubt, and carried on cutting our way through the great mountain roads of this region. On occasion the clouds were lifting and it felt more of a heavy mist falling on us, but at no time did it look like it would stop and the sun would come out. None of this took away the breathtaking scenery though. At times we could be riding on cliff edges with a steep valley laid below, and small hamlets dotted along them. Then we would be on a small flat peak, having climbed another small road to what were the tops of the foothills to the Pyrenees. If these were giving us great fun then, and in these conditions, we were in for the best time ever this week. Let's just hope the weather turns back to blue skies and sunny.

As we descended down what was to be one of our last mountain roads for the morning the mist was clearing and we could see we were entering a large open valley with a main road running through it, the N-629. Dave pulled over and we looked over the map. This main road was no use to us, as we needed to carry on heading east. Bugger, I was soaked now and we had both decided we needed to get to the hotel as soon as we could, before we both ended with a cold as well.

Dave took the BU-554, yet another of the small mountain roads, which would cut straight east, picking up the A-624, which would lead us to the autovia AP-68. Although it was a toll road for a short section, it was our quickest option to get moving towards the hotel and getting off the bikes. We worked our way through the small roads and tight corners. At one point Dave was stuck behind a car with me right behind him. It was our first traffic of the day but we could not overtake as there was a steep drop on one side of the road as we climbed and no room on the other side due to a shallow drainage channel cut into the side of the road. The car filled the road, with little more than six inches either side of it, so we were just riding behind. If nothing else, it was less stressful than cutting through the fog alone, as at least we had the car's rear lights to follow.

The car pulled over when we eventually came to a parking area at the side of the road, so we were now on our own with Dave back out in front and me doing all I could to stay with him. Finally, within ten minutes the mist was lifting, but not the rain. We could carry a little more speed, and as we started to descend once again we could see in the distance the AP-68, our new route and quicker way out of here.

We made it to the valley floor and Dave managed to take the wrong turn, so we ended up stopping to turn around. I asked if we should find another café as we had been back on the road for two hours now and I was frozen. We agreed it was a good idea, so we followed a small sign for the village of Oiardo. We were now entering the Basque country. Before too long we came across a small café on the left-hand side of the road. We were in the middle of nowhere and drenched. We pulled into the small car park, both just fell off our bikes, and headed for the safety of a dry café and to try to warm up a little.

The café was a very small place, with only five tables, each with four chairs. To the far right were four elderly locals playing cards and enjoying their coffee with brandies, and quite boisterous at it. To the left by the counter was a young couple in their early twenties I would guess, and then us two. The room fell silent as we entered. Don't ask why, but it might be that they had never seen a totally wet Lard Arse with his mate Fat Man looking like they had just survived a shipwreck and been washed up on the shore of the nearest island. Yes, we were hanging.

Jackets were off as soon as we could, and we grabbed the table right next to the two-bar electric heater hanging from the ceiling. Helmets and gloves were laid out on the table to enable everything to start drying out by the fire. I went to the counter. The guy had obviously noticed we were English, as the first thing he said as I approached was, "Mi no hablo Inglés", which translated means, "I don't speak English". So it was my Spanish once again. I ordered coffee and viewed the tapas that was sitting on the bar in a glass cabinet. There were some lovely looking egg and chorizo rolls, so I ordered two and asked if he could make them hot. That was not easy either with my limited Spanish but we managed to understand each other eventually and I sat down.

As we drank our coffees and ate our rolls, which really were lovely and tasty, I started to sort out my extremely wet gloves. By now Dave was making fun at almost every stop we had for the past two or three days, because the linings of my gloves were becoming detached, and with shovels for hands, each time I removed my hands, no matter how hard I tried, I would have the insides come out of the gloves with my hand too. Now they were wet I had no chance of getting them back together, so I would need to use the spare pair I had brought with me.

At least we were starting to cheer up. The café was great though, and we ordered another coffee and the old guys packed up and headed out. They were all looking over Dave's bike with his UK number plates. It looks like there aren't too many Brits calling into this café each day.

Time was moving on and, although we weren't dry, it had stopped raining at last. We paid and headed off to get going. With my reserve dry gloves on I felt like a new man, especially as I now had warm hands. We rode back to the toll road and the short journey south to get the N-622, then joining the A-1 autovia. This was our motorway direct route to the city of Pamplona.

It was my first time on a clear motorway since we started the journey. It was a dual carriageway and very straight. The rain had stopped now and, although it wasn't sunny, the sky was starting to brighten up as we hit the slip road on to it. The wind was also quite strong and it was gusting from our right across the motorway. Dave was still in front and I could see he was teasing me to hit some speed. Before too long we were cruising at 130–140km. It took me more than fifteen minutes to get comfortable at this speed, especially with the wind hitting us and moving us slightly to the inside of the carriageway we were on. My confidence was high though, and I was in control.

We entered a narrowing incline and the road looked to be taking a very long left turn over what could have been one to two kilometres. The wind was dying down as we entered this sheltered stretch of road and I decided I would open the throttle a bit and see if I could overtake Dave. There was no one else on the road, so I picked up the speed, and by the time I had pulled alongside, I wanted to give him the middle finger salute, but alas I didn't have the confidence to let go of the handle bars.

Dave had picked his speed up as he had seen me coming. I looked down at the speedometer and it read 179kph, or 112mph in old money. It was my fastest speed on a bike by a long way and I soon realised I'm no speed freak, so I let the bike slow down naturally, not using any brakes, pulled back in behind Dave and followed him again like the good sheep I am.

I needed fuel – well that was my excuse as to why I didn't keep on speeding past Dave – so I signalled we should pull in and Dave did so at the next service station. We had covered 65km all morning on the small mountain roads, but in the past hour we had covered 155km and now were only 100–120km from Pamplona. We both filled up, I ordered coffee and finally we could sit in the sunshine as we drank it outside the service station. It was still windy and we were both still damp but the warmth of the sunshine was raising our spirits once again.

We left the services but first had some fun in the enormous car park with the reverse steering and tight corners and building up speed as we did it. It was a good bit of fun but we couldn't stay playing like boys all day as we had plans to get the washing done in Pamplona.

It was not long, though, before we were pulling into Pamplona and we headed for the city centre signs, as our hotel was in the heart of the city. We found it very easily, and I sat outside alongside Dave's bike as he walked in and checked us in and found out where we could park the bikes. He was soon back out and we were parking in the hotel car park, situated in the basement. A quick lift journey back up to the third floor and we collapsed in our room. We were both in need of a hot shower and some fresh clothes. With a quick search of the local area on good old Google we found that there was a launderette only 500m away so, once showered, we piled all the washing into bags and set off to find it.

The place was very clean and looked new. Dave took great pleasure in making fun of me as Vanessa is one of those wonderful ladies who does everything for me. Yes, I had no idea how the washing machines worked, but thankfully Dave did. As Dave filled the washing machine up, I had lots of fun perfecting a great selfie of me holding out one of the plastic washing baskets lying around the floor and looking up to a lady that had been wallpapered on to the wall as an advert. It took a few shots before I got the size of her and me in the correct perspective but it was worth it. Now I have a great picture where I can tell everyone about how I was explaining to the lady in the launderette how the machines work. Some things please small minds as they say. Dave, however, was quite embarrassed, but who cares?

My bit of fun was over and we then moved on to the tumble dryers. I let Dave sort this out as he was very quick to insist I remain seated throughout the period when he emptied the washing machine and placed everything in the tumbler. That was fine though, as I was chatting to a local lady who thought it very amusing to see the two of us in there acting so childish and having so much fun. She explained that she had lived in the UK for two years many years ago, in the west country, which explained her great English. She was very interested to hear about our journey so far, and before too long she was wishing us the best of luck for the rest of the journey, by which time I was asking if she would like me to show her how to use the tumble dryer too. That's when Dave dragged me out and we both bid our farewells to her.

I was feeling in a mischievous mood by now. It was back to the hotel to drop the clothes off, but it was only just after 6pm and way too early to go out to eat. We were both having fun today, and particularly enjoying the early finish, even if we had started off like drowned rats all morning.

I opened up my tablet to see just how we could sort out a new intercom now we were back in Spain. We had decided that we would be staying for a two-night period at our next stop, but not camping, as it was too chilly for Dave and his tent wasn't in the best of conditions after his drunken evening on the port. If I signed up to the Amazon something or other, I could get free delivery anywhere in Spain and use the drop and collect system.

Dave came up with a great central town of Java as our destination for next two days. I then looked to find the replacement item to get our intercoms back up and working. I could have it delivered, but as it was after 6pm it would not be there until the Wednesday afternoon, not the Tuesday, which was tomorrow. I had a choice of four different places to have the delivery sent and I plumped for the one that was most central to the town centre, and having looked the place up it was open until 8pm every evening, so time would not be a problem. Order placed for the intercom, as well as the pick-up point, and it was time to think about our stomachs.

Dave had just received a call from Caroline so I headed down to the bar for a quick refreshment on my own to see what was on offer. It was a lovely cold Estrella beer, and guess what, it came with two small tapas, a small hot chorizo in the smallest bread roll I've ever seen and a mixture of three cheeses, all stacked on a piece of cucumber and held together with a green plastic party stick. By the time Dave came down and found me I was just ordering another beer so I doubled the order and we now had some different tapas to sample, one fish tapas and what looked like croquettes. Dave had the two fish ones, as I don't do fish, and I had what I thought was the best of the deal, two ham croquettes. We could have stayed there all evening on the beer and tapas, but it wasn't substantial enough for us, with the amount of beer we would have had to drink just say we had had a good meal that night, so we drank up and headed into town.

We had been discussing the tapas bar that was near the launderette earlier, and as it was quite chilly and very windy tonight we decided it would be a good place to start. I found out later on my return to Marbella that the tapas restaurant here was part of a chain, the restaurant Montaditos, and definitely worth a visit. We ordered beer. Neither of the girls behind the counter spoke English, even in this university town. No problem though, and it was my Spanish once again to the rescue, asking whether they had an English menu, which arrived with two large beers. The Estrella beer was starting to grow on us, although at 5.4%, large beers were to be savoured not demolished.

The English menu was a photocopy, I believe made by Google Translate, and it was so small I had to use Dave's glasses to read the text. I went up to the bar and I ordered three tapas each, a mixture between pork belly, chorizo sausages, different cheeses and egg. Ten minutes later, the lady from the counter was tapping me on the shoulder to tell me I was being called to collect my food. We had two large plates of tapas to devour. Wow, great value, as the cost of both plates were only €6.50, yet another bargain dinner.

Regardless of who ordered what, we were sampling each tapas and enjoying yet another evening. We did order another plate of tapas, but only four dishes this time, and another beer. This time, we were both listening for my name to be called once it was ready. We had a lovely time and once again the clock was ticking down to another late night for the two of us, so we headed back. We thought about the hotel bar, but decided against it and were tucked up in bed by 10pm. Two dirty stop-outs – what will our wives think!

Chapter 15

A Sweet Soul Start with a Biblical Ride Through the Pyrenees

Tuesday, 25 September

23°C – clear skies all day but a chill in the air

219km travelled today

After a wet start yesterday, today was the complete opposite, clear blue skies and the sun beaming down on us as we headed out. No breakfast booked, we were going to eat on the run today, especially after all the tapas the night before.

We rode out of the hotel car park at 8am, and were surprised at just how cold it was, 7°C, and with a slight breeze too. It was a straightforward ride out of the city as we were early and there was no traffic on the roads. We were heading north-west and in need of fuel before too long as yesterday's motorway speedy hour had almost emptied our tanks. As we filled up with fuel, the feeling this morning could not have been any different than it had been the day before.

I entered the office to pay for my fuel, with a boisterous "hola, buenos día" in my best Spanish, closely followed by a "good morning gentlemen" in English, just to make sure they did not think I was Spanish. Not as if that would ever happen, with my poor Spanish. I was greeted by two guys who were slightly surprised at the village idiot who had just walked in (yes me!). The guy to the right greeted me with a rather sarcastic, "Hola, buenas día, mucha calor hoy", translated as "Hello, good day, it's very hot today". This guy was on my wavelength and we had a few moments banter as I started to say it was very, very hot and too much sun today, as I paid. Dave was all a little lost as to what was happening, but after thirty-five years he's used to me making a fool of us both when we're out together. It's happened once or twice before.

We were back on the bikes and the temperature was rising now to 12°C, a modest rise but you could feel a little warmth growing. We were riding on the N-135 and on the lookout for breakfast as we started to climb into the rolling hills and mountains of the Pyrenees.

It was only another forty minutes before we were entering the third village of the day looking for a café. Espinal is a chocolate-box village built with granite cornerstones to each corner of every house and property, and whitewashed rendered walls. The whole village must get painted every year as everything looks so fresh and picturesque. I spotted a café on my left as we slowly rode through. Dave had missed it, but we were eager to get breakfast before we entered the French side of the ride today, so exiting the village he pulled over and I told him we should head back, which we did. We parked the bikes in a small square, which was no bigger than a tennis court and full of people sitting drinking coffee and eating pastries. Dave grabbed one of the spare tables and I went in to get coffee and a sandwich for breakfast.

What happened next was to stay with me all day. As I walked into the café, there were a good eight to ten people in front of me or just waiting to pay. I could see an elderly guy in his mid-sixties behind the counter with a silver-haired ponytail. He was wearing a leather waistcoat and shirt and tie. The counter was full of dirty cups and saucers and a young lady was trying to order, in German, two black coffees.

Just as I was beginning to think of maybe not staying, there was a familiar tune starting up on the radio and the man serving turned the speaker up louder. It was Arthur Conley singing 'Sweet Soul Music', an absolute soul classic from 1967. Now the guy serving was starting to strut his stuff along the counter, and as he did, he was cleaning away cups and saucers, taking money and ringing up the till, all whilst jiving away and singing to this classic song. He was even putting a few 360-degree turns in and an occasional right-hand high jive, just like John Travolta would do years after this number had been released in *Saturday Night Fever*. This was a great start to breakfast and I was going nowhere until the song was over. Everyone was in a great mood and the guy had us all in the palms of his hands. Magical even now to just remember that few minutes in the café.

Eventually I managed to order coffees and two chocolate-covered pastries, paid and left the café. As I was walking out I could hear the Aretha Franklin hit 'I Say a Little Prayer' starting up and I could only imagine the guy going through all his moves once again and enjoying his morning behind the bar. If you're ever in the village of Espinal and in need of a good coffee and light entertainment, hopefully you will get what we did. Just pop into the Gran Café Tapas Bar, Plaza Teobaldo. Sometimes such simple memories are absolutely priceless and this one will be with me and told several times in my lifetime.

Time to move on as it was almost 10am now. The day was about to get even better as the route Dave had planned was awesome. We carried on following the N-135 north to France.

The road was a real challenge for me, and what we had experienced previously was child's stuff compared to this. We turned right on to a small road, the D-302, that would take us due east, and the fun just carried on as we were climbing for over forty minutes on quality mountain roads, enclosed at times in thick forestry either side, which cooled the temperature down. But then, without any warning, we would be out into bright sunshine and steep inclines either side of the road as we wound our way up. On occasion we would have a small stream running alongside the road, then it would disappear and off we would go again on steep inclines and sharp twisty roads, weaving left and right, as I learned the art of motorcycling. This was such fun.

Before too long we had made it to the top of this section of road and were looking out over a large plain, with several bird spotters all set up, just like they were back at Tarifa the week before. We parked the bikes carefully at the side of the road and headed along a short pass on foot just to take in the views, looking down one side into Spain and on the other side were the French Pyrenees, just stunning. As someone who has lived for over twelve years in the Austrian Alps, this was up there with the best scenery Europe has to offer.

After fifteen minutes and a few pictures, we mounted and started our descent over the opposite side of the pass. This descent was even steeper than the journey up, but what a ride down. There was still no traffic and Dave decided he needed to lose altitude as soon as possible and enjoy his holiday too, so he left me while he raced his way around the endless twists and turns ahead of us. I pootled on at my own speed and was enjoying the whole experience just as much. The rule was to keep going on the same road until I found Dave parked up waiting for me, so it was several Hamlets later that I met up with him again. I had a huge Cheshire Cat grin all over my face, or at least it felt like it, as I had passed my first morning on the big boy roads up here in the mountains and was extremely pleased with myself.

But now time was pushing on and it was just before 2pm. We were following a river, the Gave de Sainte-Engrâce, through a very steep gorge. The water was the most amazing turquoise blue that really was inviting, but with the temperature at only 23°C now, there was no way we were jumping in. We pulled over right in the middle of nowhere on a corner with a small mountain restaurant to get a drink and something to eat.

This was to be a meal to remember. There was no place to sit at the front of the restaurant as it was full with what looked like locals, so we entered and were met by a very lively lady dressed in a tight-fitting basque and long traditional dress that covered up little and pushed the rest out for all to see. She did, however, speak great English and directly welcomed us to the restaurant. Her mother owned the place and she worked there alongside her younger brother, the chef. We ordered coffee and a sparkling water and she told us to sit outside in the sunshine at the side of the place, where there were more tables.

She brought over the drinks and a menu and asked if we wanted to eat, then explained they had two specials of the day. One was French Basque omelette, made with four eggs, all fresh from their chickens, and filled with tomatoes, onions and diced pieces of their own smoked ham. That was Dave's choice, while I went for the second special, which was pork belly from wild boar, with fried eggs and chips. She took the order and moments later an elderly guy came and sat at the table next to us, dressed in biking gear too. He introduced himself as Folkart, from Keil or a small village close to it. He was on his way to Spain for the winter months. He and his wife had a motor home and were taking a few weeks out to enjoy the journey down to their winter destination.

He had a rather old light-blue metallic 1992 BMW 1100cc cruising bike that was in great condition. We explained our journey and he was enthralled by the whole idea of circumnavigating the Iberian coastline and a week out for fun here in the Pyrenees too.

Our dinner arrived and we tucked in and polished off some really great home cooking. The day was getting better and better, and we had a new biker friend too. We wished our new friend a great time on his holidays and he bid us the same friendly farewell.

After leaving the restaurant, as we meandered through the tight twisty road, we could see to our right the Gorges de Kakuetta. The river had been dammed for hydroelectric power and turned into a very long but not too wide reservoir that was the most beautiful of colours. Each side of the reservoir was so steep it was almost vertical, on one side of which we were hanging on to on the bikes, making sure there were no mistakes here, as I would hate to think just how deep the water was at this point down below us.

As we carried on we started to open up into a wider valley, and as we came sharply around a right-hand corner just outside a small hamlet we were met by a flock of sheep in the middle of the road. Each sheep had a bell around its neck, and the sound was deafening, like an orchestra trying to tune up prior to their performance. The flock filled the road completely and, with nowhere to go, we were stuck behind them. At the back of the flock were three shepherds and I could also make out several more along the sides of the flock all the way down the road. The flock must have been 10m wide and over 250m long, and there really were thousands of them.

Finally, one of the shepherds motioned that we should follow him. Dave was in front and me following as usual. The shepherd took his long staff and another from one of his colleagues and started to jog through the flock, with each step smashing his staff on the ground as he shouted at the sheep. Left, right, jog and shout, with Dave close behind him and me only a metre away from Dave's back wheel. This really was a biblical scene, like when Moses held out his staff and the Red Sea was parted. The Israelites walked on the exposed dry ground and crossed the separated Red Sea, just like we were by following this shepherd through the flock of sheep. Let's just hope that we won't end up like the Egyptian army, as when Moses moved his staff after the Israelites had crossed, the sea closed, drowning the entire army.

It seemed like a lifetime but it must have only been a minute or two and we were through. We had just experienced something that can only happen but once in a lifetime. We had never seen so many sheep, and riding through them was an experience in itself, especially with our biblical shepherd. I can still hear the sound of those bells now, and yet again this story will be told many times over in my coming years I'm sure.

Heading off, we wanted to get a picture of the sheep to prove just how big the flock was, so we pulled up about a kilometre away and parked the bikes. We were on a bridge and looking straight back at the road we had just come from. Just at that moment we could hear a huge racket and once again bells banging away behind us. It turned out to be a small side road just to the other side of the bridge where the bikes were parked. There was a herd of cows coming down this road and heading straight towards the bikes and we only had about 200m before they were swallowed up by the cattle.

We forgot about the photos of the sheep and ran like hell to mount the bikes and get away before any damage was done or we were made into a filling of a sheep and cattle sandwich on this road. I've no idea how many cattle were coming down the road but we could see at least a hundred and fifty before the road was lost inside a dense thick forest. We mounted and moved off in time, not really knowing what had just happened since dinner. We pulled over about ten minutes later just to have a chat and get our breath back. Just how big was today's tale going to be?

We pushed on once again and picked up the N-134 as we entered back into the Spanish side of the day's adventures. We were an hour away from our destination for the next two nights, the city of Jaca. Dave thought it a good idea for one last small mountain road, so he took us out to the left on to the N-330a, which was a small road where any car, even the smallest, would find it very hard to stay on the black stuff, but it was great fun. We ended the day with more adrenaline-pumping corners, steep descents and picture opportunities of some wonderful alpine scenery.

It was not long before we were in the city and heading for the Gran Hotel de Jaca, right in the centre and close to all that this city had to offer. Dave checked us in whilst I looked over the two Irish bikes parked in the car park. One was the same as my bike, a Yamaha Tracer, the other was a large Ducati, I've no idea what, being the novice I am, but it was big.

After checking into a very nice clean room, then having a shower, I caught up on my journal for the day. Our first job then was to find the drop-off place in the town where I would collect the intercom the following day. Having searched the streets for a while thinking we were looking for a UPS depot or small shop, I ended up spotting two ladies in a shop talking, so I walked in and asked them if they knew where I should be. The two ladies, one blonde and one brunette, not that I can remember too much about them (that comment is for my wife if she's reading), turned out to be very attractive and more than happy to just drop everything and come for a walk down the street to ask in each shop whether they knew the place I was looking for. We eventually entered a cigar shop and the guy knew just what we were looking for and directed us to a small shop a few doors down. I thanked the two ladies for being so helpful and they both smiled and wished me good luck.

Entering the shop was a real experience. This was not any old shop but a shop for ladies of a certain age and size – this is most probably the best way for me to describe it. Three ladies were in the shop, two looking through several sets of large knickers, just like the ones Bridget Jones was famous for in *Bridget Jones's Diary*. The knickers had been placed on the counter by the middle-aged lady behind the counter. The last lady, who was slightly larger than the others, was inspecting something I can only describe as my great grandmother's underwear, a huge all-in-one elasticated garment, quite scary for me as a fifty-year-old, if I say so myself.

I introduced myself, trying as hard as I could not to stare. I asked whether the lady serving spoke English, which came back with a straight no. The three ladies shopping now had me as their main attraction in the shop, as I tried to explain that I was expecting a delivery via Amazon drop-off, but not today, tomorrow.

It developed into many hand signals and Spanglish (English and Spanish mixed together) words made up as I went along, before either of us knew what I was talking about. The ladies, bless them, had stopped shopping for the next Bridget Jones film and were doing their best to translate all of this from my English, which none of them spoke, into Spanish to the lady serving. It was just like a great big game of charades but with the ability to talk; however, no one knew what I was talking about.

Having shown the lady my order from Amazon that I had on my phone, she checked what she had already and told me to come back tomorrow to collect it. I bid goodnight to each of the ladies, who all in turn wished me buenos noches (goodnight) too, as everyone went about their business again with big smiles, all aimed at the stupid Englishman who had just left.

After this I needed a beer, so we headed straight into the first bar we found, right on the main high street and with several people in it. We only had one beer, as the time was getting on for 8pm now and this bar was about to close, don't ask why, but it closed and we left. We were on the hunt for food as we headed back down the high street to retrace our tracks from earlier to several restaurants we had seen whilst looking for the UPS shop.

Eventually, after entering three other restaurants and seeing they were packed, we settled on a small bar with a huge glass food case of tapas running along the counter. There were lots of full tables but room at the bar for me and Dave. We only wanted a snack after our big lunch in the mountains so we ordered a couple of draft beers and asked the young lady behind the counter if she could explain what all the different tapas were. She was great, and although she spoke no English, she was more than willing to put the time in to understand my poor Spanish, so we ordered one portion to share of wild boar pork belly, homemade chorizo sausage cut up into small slices, deep-fried boar lips and a large Spanish meatball with gravy.

I had to explain to the lady that when she kept pointing two fingers at me to ask if I wanted one portion or two she should bear in mind that the English took this as an insult. With a slightly red face she finally understood and we had ordered a meal to be shared and fit for kings. We ordered another beer, and the food arrived only five minutes later, and with a large bread basket full of crispy French stick.

We munched our way through the meal and a couple more beers whilst having the odd conversation with the young lady, as she kept enquiring if the food was good. It had been a very eventful day and we had so much to talk about for today's travels. How were we ever going to top today?

Chapter 16

The Heights of the Pyrenees Through Spain and France

Wednesday, 26 September

28°C – clear blue skies

278km travelled today

We decided to not take the breakfast option in the hotel, deciding instead to explore once again the cafés and local pastries that had worked well so far. As we were staying a second night, we headed off at 9am after removing all luggage from the bikes. We were all stripped down to the bare bike and man for today's adventures.

It was only 9°C as we headed out and the plan was to follow our noses this morning and just have some fun. We would keep on the twisty roads with no specific plan other than to enjoy the ride. We took the E-7 out of Jaca for a short 10km ride along the motorway, then collected the N-260 north into the mountains. Within thirty minutes we were then heading up the small A-136 leading towards the French border and some of the larger ski areas in this region, such as El Formigal.

The riding was once again awesome and I was really enjoying this. After nine days of being a novice I really did think I was starting to be very natural at handling the bike, especially on these quite demanding mountain roads. As we travelled north we were all alone once again, with no traffic. We stopped and pulled over to take pictures of a large reservoir, the Embalse de Búbal, that we were hugging tight as the road pushed us higher into the mountains.

I could see El Formigal in the distance before we arrived. We rode up past the town, and the ski region was over to the left, with all the redundant chairlifts standing dormant in the late summer sunshine. Heading back into the town, which was less than a kilometre away, we parked up and headed for the only café that was open, which had a small parking area. Dave headed for a table in the sunshine as it was quite cool in the shade, while I went inside and ordered coffee and two chorizo omelettes for breakfast.

The guy spoke some English and I asked about the ski region and how high we were, to be told that we were 1,550m above sea level and by all accounts there was a good covering of snow every year too during the winter ski season. The region looked great. As I live every winter in the Austrian ski resort of the Wildkogel, I'm a lover of winter sports but have never skied the Pyrenees, so this place was now on my to-do list.

After our stop we carried on through the Sallent de Gállego pass, the main pass from Spain into France. When I say it's the main pass, it's been there for a lifetime, although the roads are very small and it's quite a desolate area up there. We stopped after only forty minutes after breakfast at the summit of the pass at Frontera del Portalet to take in the views, and what views we had. Looking back into Spain it was a large desolate landscape, quite dry and brown, and with very little greenery until you could see the lowlands in the distance. France, however, was such a different view. We were looking over the mountain tops and peaks, counting the valleys as they cut their way through the rugged landscape to form this beautiful region.

After a few more pictures we were off again, following the roads down through the French side of today's journey. There were small ski resorts scattered around for the next hour, and the roads were now very steep and extremely twisty, making them difficult for me to handle. I knew what was coming as I could now see for almost 10km into the distance and the windy road seemed to be skipping along the mountains we were yet to travel through. Yes, it was Dave time again and he was off to get his twisty fix. I'm so glad he had the confidence to leave me, to be honest, as I'm not sure I would have in his shoes.

I was enjoying the day though, and when Dave disappeared it's not that I should try to speed up and follow him, as I was resigned to the fact that I'm a novice and he is by far a more experienced rider than I will probably ever be. You can't blame him though, as there was still no traffic, and you could see the road for kilometres, cutting around the mountains, and for at least 400m in front of you, as we made our way.

After an hour and a half of climbing summits on the bikes and then descending for it all to start again and again, we were starting to see more forested areas, and this time there was an autumnal feel to the region. We were in France, not Spain, and it all looked a little tired now when we rode through the villages and hamlets.

We stopped off for a coffee in a small spa town of Valvital – Thermes des Eaux Bonnes, situated on a steep hillside and surrounded by a thick forest. The town just appeared on us. We could see no sign of life anywhere, but pulled up to the largest of the hotels on offer and entered the place. A middle-aged lady appeared and spoke great English, and she summoned a young guy to come and serve coffee to us. The place was just like the village and region, run down and in need of a facelift. Without being too down on the place, it gave the slight impression of a Faulty Towers hotel. We stayed for only one coffee, and at €8.40 for the two coffees, we would not be back for another.

Heading out on the D-918, we were now climbing very steeply, rising and encircling the town we had just left, heading up through the top of the Eaux Bonnes pass, and the views were just stunning. Once again this region had differing views to offer. We stopped and looked down from the side of the road into deep valleys of shale and rock, with little vegetation now as we were so high. We could see the road we had travelled up cutting its way into the hard rock and traversing around the mountainsides for miles as it made its way to the point we were standing at. Once again a memory that will stay with me for many years to come.

We carried on and through the village of Béost, now heading up past the village of Gourette, still being wowed by the never-ending views of the rooftop of this lovely region. We headed east for the next hour, staying with the D-918, which was a ride to remember. In the whole day we had seen no more than six cars and three bikes on the road since leaving Jaca.

Descending now, we entered the French town of Pierrefitte-Nestalas, which is small but very pretty. We had by now no idea of our exact proximity to Jaca and needed to take a coffee and work out our route back, so we pulled over into a roadside café and parked the bikes alongside an old tractor in the small industrial area next to the café. We both sat down as a lady from inside the café came straight out and asked what we would like. She spoke really good English, which was a relief, as I speak no French and Dave is still trying to master English when he has to.

As she walked back inside I could not help but wonder whether she had bought the short cocktail dress she was wearing back in the 1980s, when short dresses with shoulder padding were all the fashion. She was the right age to have done so, but then again, who am I to judge the poor lady, as I at fifty-one still have Vanessa dressing me, as she has absolutely no faith that I actually understand any form or meaning of the word fashion. Not that she really understands the actual fashion-breaking areas that I actually move in, especially with my bright-green ski jacket this year, and orange salopettes. I think it's ground-breaking fashion for the coming ski season, but everyone else seems to laugh at me!

We had 124km to travel back to Jaca, and it was now 2.30pm, so today was to be a long day, but definitely not a boring one. We finished up our coffee and mounted up again for the ride back. Still heading east, to pick up one of the main valleys back down towards Jaca, we were climbing again, as we had to get back up and over the mountain range. No more than twenty minutes into the ride we stumbled upon a huge herd of cows; you really just could not make this story up. It was just like the day before when we ran into the flock of sheep, only these animals were five times bigger and if they hit you they were going to do you some damage.

The herd meandered down the road for over 150m, not as big as the herd yesterday but just as loud, with their bells clanging away as they stumbled down the road. At the back where we were, there was a small Ford Fiesta, with two herdsmen walking in front of the car at the back of the herd, again both with large staffs. The car was beckoned through using the same jogging routine as was used yesterday. We were stuck right on the car's rear bumper, with only a half metre to spare. We were not going to be singled out by these bloody animals. It was a rather scary affair, as the driver of the car in front was, I think, more scared than we were of the cows, as he kept hitting the brakes every few moments. We made it through though, and once again we had another great story to tell, albeit not as much fun as yesterday as we were now getting old hat at taking on mountain herds whilst on the bikes.

We were through quickly enough and soon overtook the Fiesta on our ascent as we climbed up through the Arcizans-Dessus pass. We were looking down to our right-hand side to a huge gorge, whilst clinging tight to the steep slopes on our left. There was the occasional car in the afternoon, but if in total I said five cars, I might be exaggerating the fact. We entered a large plateau as we closed in on the top of the pass and it was covered with flocks of sheep, herds of cows and scores of donkeys all grassing away as we, the intruders of their world, just rode on through.

Time was moving on now and we had not eaten all day since breakfast, so we pushed on, but I knew I needed to eat soon. As we turned south on the French road, the D-173, Dave was off. It was Dave time again, and why not? We were on a large dual carriageway now with almost no traffic and all he could see was fun, fun, fun.

It was another hour before we were back in Spain and on the main A-138 heading south and out of the mountains. We stopped in the village of Escalona, with a large river dominating one side of the dual carriageway we were travelling on. We pulled over for a sandwich and a drink. It had been a long day so far with good kilometres and lots of fun again. There was a huge chunk of rock dominating the village on the opposite side of the road. When the waitress came over I asked if she spoke English and the reply was, in Spanish, "Un poco", (a little), but she never said a word in English so it was down to my Spanish yet again.

It was a quick pitstop and back on to the road south. Again Dave kept heading off and I don't blame him. My speed was getting better on these roads after so many cornering manoeuvres over the past few days, and it was never too long now that Dave had to wait for me, and on most occasions I could just make him out in the distance.

Within an hour we were back on the E-7 and coming into Jaca after yet another great day out. It was now just after 5pm so it was a shower, shave and write the journal up before heading out to collect the new intercom that had hopefully arrived. We both fancied the tapas bar we had been to the night before, so our night was all arranged.

It was 7pm before we finally headed into town. The first job was to collect my new intercom, which had hopefully been delivered. It was only a ten-minute walk now as we knew where the shop was, and Dave stood outside like my bouncer as I went inside for another round of Spanglish conversation with the lady in the shop. She recognised me as I entered and gave a large smile. She was serving a customer and broke away to pop into the rear room to collect a small box that had my name and parcel reference on it.

Job done, I had a new intercom; I had my safety blanket back and I could, as I knew I would, annoy the hell out of Dave now as we rode the rest of the journey. I thanked the lady and we retraced our route back to have a couple of beers in a German pub we had noticed on the way to the UPS shop earlier. We both ordered a Warsteiner beer, thinking it would be pulled from the draft pump that was right in front of us at the bar. It soon turned out there were no German beers in the place but lots of empty bottles on show on every shelf in the bar, so we settled for a couple of Estrella beers on draft and had a good chat about today's events once again. Our mileage was not huge over the past two days but it had been full-on concentration with the number of mountain roads and trails we had taken on. Dave was as pleased as punch, as I was too, that we were on this journey.

It was not long before we were on our way for round two in the local tapas bar we had eaten at the night before. I stayed with the pork belly and meatballs tonight, while Dave dived into three fish dishes, the only one of which he knew being octopus. The service was just as warm as the night before. The young lady recognised us and we were even asked if we enjoyed the day out on our bikes. However, to go into detail was way over my Spanish level so we just nodded and said, "Sì". How could we explain all we had seen and done with our basic Spanish and hand signals?

After another lovely evening and maybe one beer too many we headed off for bed. It was past 10pm and we are animals of habit, who liked to be tucked up in bed by this time of night. Let's face it, we are in our fifties now (Dave is almost sixty though) so god knows what we will be like in our sixties?

Chapter 17

Last Full Day's pleasure in the Mountains with a Donkey to Snuggle up To!

Thursday, 27 September

27°C – clear blue skies

241km travelled today

It was another cool start to this morning, only 10°C as we checked out and loaded the cases on to the bikes. I had a chat with one of the Irish guys whose bikes we had spotted when we arrived two days ago, and he was intrigued by our journey. Turns out he was doing a similar tour but in the opposite direction, the east coast, then along the Costa del Sol and up the west border of Spain. He knew the dealer I had hired my bike from, as two years before he hired a bike from them too. I wished him luck and we were on our way.

The intercoms were working fine, and we now had a new routine each time we mounted the bike to ensure they were working. I felt a little more secure knowing I could at least have a chat with Dave, especially going through the towns, which would make life much easier.

Today's plan was to head north-east in the direction of Andorra, again another region I had never visited, but it was on our hit-list of places to visit. We were hoping to find a hotel not too far from it by mid-afternoon so we could have a bit of a chill this afternoon, as we were now almost two weeks on the road.

Retracing our steps from our ride home the day before, we were heading back up the N-260, and the plan was to get close to, or into the town of Boltaña for breakfast. It was a great ride, with a wide single carriageway road followed by sections of dual carriageway and endless long swooping corners bearing right, then left, just to keep us amused as we picked up speed.

Boltaña was quite a large place compared to how it looked on the map. We pulled up at a café with chairs and tables outside, and as Dave made a call to Caroline to wish her a happy birthday, I nipped inside and ordered two coffees and the traditional toast and olive oil breakfast. On my return I called Vanessa to see if she had had a good time too. She had returned home that morning from her safari holiday with her girlfriend and it was good to catch up, even if it was only for a few minutes.

Breakfast arrived and we finished off the toast and coffee. Across the road was a very small bakery, which had the smallest of shopfront windows. There were people in and out the whole time we had been enjoying breakfast. I nudged Dave and told him I needed a sugar rush now and he agreed that he too could do with a little more to eat. I paid the bill and we headed over to see what was on offer. The window displayed only bread and rolls and looked more like a permanent display of their fare, so we headed in.

Inside was a real Aladdin's cave of pastries and artisan bread. There was a rather long thin pastry that looked like a two-foot pizza with sugar sprinkled all over it. I asked what it was and the lady explained it was a local speciality called tortilla cristal. We ordered some, plus two of the largest chocolate croissants we had ever seen – this was really going to be a sugar rush. Heading back to the bikes, we sat and ate the croissants and tortilla cristal, which were both lovely, then it was time to move on and see just what this day had in store for us.

The road carried on with endless long corners and very little traffic. We were carrying some good speed now. Having the intercoms did have some effect on this, as Dave was riding about 500m in front of me and would tell me what direction was coming up and whether the road had a slight, normal or sharp corner, just to give me a little time to adjust myself. It sounds basic but I did find it helpful, and this way I could just about keep Dave in my sights; either that or he was holding back to let me.

Within a half an hour we were in a very narrow gorge for about 10km, heading towards the village of Foradada del Toscar. It looked great fun on the map, and the map was right – tight corners followed by long straights before yet another chicane to contend with before it all started over and over again. As we exited Foradada del Toscar, we were climbing and heading into small tunnels no more than 300m long, then out again into the sunlight to see the steep gorge below. We were almost able to touch the other side of the gorge it was so narrow. We stopped a couple of times just for pictures and to look down to the river below. We were extremely high here and the views through the gorge were great.

We were soon through the villages of Campo and Castejón de Sos, and this was now turning out to be an adventure once again. We still had no traffic to contend with as we were climbing steeply continuously, and the road could be seen for as far as the eye could see into the distance. What had started out as a narrow gorge had now opened up into a huge wide valley and we were climbing to its summit far into the distance.

It was Dave time again, but today I had the advantage of being told over our intercoms that he was going, and it gave me great pleasure for the first time to be able to wish him good luck and to enjoy himself. I was going fast enough and enjoying the roads, and it wasn't long before Dave was just a speck in the distance, climbing up to the top of this pass.

As we rode over the other side of the pass, having reached the summit, we hit a never-ending supply of 180-degree corners, the first two of which I nailed absolutely perfectly, and I was shouting and singing away to myself. We then had a short steep descent for about a kilometre, then into a meandering ride, slowly descending for over thirty minutes. I caught up with Dave, or he slowed down for me, and we had a photo stop. We both had great big smiles over our faces, reminiscing about the road we had just taken and the fun both of us had had for the last hour.

Heading off, Dave told me to head out in front. We were to be carrying on straight for another hour or so and heading for the signs to El Pont de Suert. We were an hour away from this destination and in no hurry to make it. I fully enjoyed my time out in front, very conscious that Dave was behind, and having to keep reminding myself it was not a race today. All I needed to do was keep it simple and nail the corners but not carry too much speed at any time. Again and again we were hitting great 180s and sometimes the occasional larger sweeping corner.

Heading out of the village of El Pont de Suert, we were still on the N-260 and now heading south. Dave was back in front and we were still having the ride of our lives on such wonderful roads. We stopped for a coffee and a drink when we arrived at the town of El Pont de Claverol, with the time getting on for 2pm now. Parking the bikes right outside a café on the main road, we were surrounded by Catalonian flags draped from almost every window sill along this main road. All the street lights and telegraph posts had yellow ribbons attached, and opposite the café was an industrial building that had eleven people's faces spray-painted on to the walls. We were to find out later that these eleven people were or had been imprisoned earlier in the year after Catalonia had voted to leave Spain and become an independent country. This was a scene that would be seen for the next four days, and we would later realise just how big the state of Catalonia is.

We grabbed a table outside. Neither of us was hungry but I went in and ordered coffee and sparkling waters for the both of us. As we drank our coffee Dave searched for a hotel for the night. We were heading north now to the town of Sort, and we were only about one hour away so we would hopefully have a chilled afternoon to unwind. After a second coffee we headed off for Sort, staying with the N-260 and following the river La Noguera Pallaresa. It was another lovely fast dual carriageway most of the way, with sections of single-file road in places.

By 3.30pm we were riding along the river into Sort. Just as we could see the buildings of the town ahead, about 100m in front of Dave we could see a red kite hovering only about 10m above the road. As we got closer, the kite dived down, then held its position only about 4m above us as we rode past it, slightly to our right-hand side, just above the river bed. What a lovely sight to finish the day.

Looking for our hotel now, we found it right on the main road only a kilometre on from our bird-spotting. It looked out over the river. We parked the bikes and headed inside to check in. I think the hotel was more of a hostel for children's activity holidays. It was a bit of a shock to have two donkeys with big smiling faces painted on the walls of our room. Let's just hope we don't have too many beers tonight and want to take them out for a ride. We both took a shower and chilled out for an hour. It was nice to have an early finish at last. Tomorrow would be our last day in the mountains, as we were to head up into Andorra then start to head back to the Spanish eastern coastline and the journey back to finish this wonderful journey.

It was getting on for 6pm now so we took a walk down to the river, then back up through the town to see just what was in this place. We stopped off for a beer at one of the two bars that were open, and decided that this is where we would eat this evening, but not this early or we would end up in bed by 7.30pm. So we walked back to the hotel, stopping off in one of the bakeries on the way to pick up a couple of Spanish pasties, or empanadas as they are called, and a slice of pizza each. We were both starving as we had had nothing to eat since breakfast that morning.

After a lie down once again to rest our tired bodies, we headed back to our destination for dinner at 8pm. We went inside this time as the wind was blowing quite hard and it was getting chilly. We were welcomed back by a young lady who had served us earlier, who spoke good Spanish but came from Romania and had been working there in the bar for three years. We had a couple of beers and ordered three tapas dishes each; no fish today, it was all pork, omelette or cheese, again with a basket of bread, and we were two happy bunnies munching away and washing it down with a beer. We knew this must be more of a holiday destination when we asked for the bill and it came to €38, not exactly the value for money we had been getting over recent days but it was lovely food and the beer as always was great.

We headed back to the hotel, taking the route through the main high street to do a little window shopping on the way back. The wind was getting even stronger now and there was a real bite in the air. Arriving back at the hotel we hit the sack straight away. I caught up on my journal and we both stuck our intercoms on charge, trying not to disturb the donkeys as it was now getting late. It could have been worse though, as the room next to us was full of pigs on the walls – now they do make   lots   of   noise!

Chapter 18

A Toll-free to Andorra, and it's Those Bloody Germans Again

Friday, 28 September

31°C – clear blue skies

343km travelled today

We were both awake by 7am, and we laid there just discussing the past few days and the wonderful time we had had, firstly getting to the Pyrenees on our first week's travel, then the past four days in the hills and mountains, with all the fun that it had brought. Again we had no set destination other than we wanted to visit Andorra, as neither of us had been there before. From there we would probably end up heading into France to get one of the main routes south back to find our Spanish coastline for the journey homeward bound.

We sat down for breakfast at 9am. There was no rush and we had earned another lazy day, or morning anyway. It was a great spread too, with pastries of all sizes covered with either sugar or chocolate, cakes and a chocolate fountain. Now you don't see them every day at a breakfast table. There were also sliced hams and salamis, various cheeses and all kinds of different artisan rolls and bread to choose from. But for me it was bacon with a couple of fried eggs to start. We decided, as it was such a good spread, that we would tank up now for the day with food and skip dinner. Dave was of the same idea too, hot food first, followed by a few cheese and salami slices and a couple of rolls, with tons of butter, all finished off with a couple of pastries and cakes dipped in chocolate sauce. All this washed down with an endless supply of hot fresh coffee – now that is a real man's breakfast. Just hope Vanessa's not reading this!

By 10am we were on the road, all checked out and heading towards the province of Andorra. It was first left over the river to exit Sort, then take the road north, and we would be back on the N-260 once again through to Andorra. The roads were deserted and again great quality black stuff beneath us. Dave was in front, as team leaders do, and we had the intercoms switched on. We were pushing the speed for the first hour as we started, just as we had finished the day before, having fun and attacking endless right-hand and left-hand 180-degree turns, which were coming at us from everywhere.

At times I will admit Dave had me on the edge of my comfort zone as he pressed hard for his fun and I hung in behind him trying to keep pace. At fourteen days into my motorcycling career though, I'm proud to say I was behind him, even if most of the time it was some distance behind. Being able to keep up with Dave for a good period of time helped me look at his entrance and exit points to the corners, which helped me adjust to improve my ride. It was that time again though, as I had a quick statement coming over the intercom, "It's twisty time", and Dave was off. No need for me to even try to keep up with him, so I set about trying to perfect some of what we had been on all morning and looking hard at my entrance and exit positions, whilst trying to hold a good speed.

It was only three of four minutes after Dave had disappeared that I took on too much on a right-hand corner. It was not that I was too fast or in the wrong position, but there was a large blister running right in my riding line, only about six feet long and maybe three inches wide, but my back wheel went over it and nudged it as I hugged the corner. My speed was only about 45kph as it was a very tight 180-degree plus corner, but it made the back end jump what felt like two feet in the air. In all honesty it was over before it had even started but

I had lost a little confidence and learned a lesson too – I'm a beginner so don't try too hard.

It didn't stop the fun though, as we were climbing and having to take on never-ending 180-degree corners every 200–300m. Then we would have a short section of dual carriageway, where Dave would ease up a little, I could close up on him and get him back into my view, and it would all start over again.

It was on a really large right-hander just at the end of a dual carriageway section that we dived down, descending quite steeply to the left. You could see the road meander all the way around to the right then around a large inlet in the mountainside. Dave was coming out of this huge corner away to my right, and I could see him way in the distance. I set my position and entered this corner of fun. I could see three or four motorcycles approaching me from behind in my rear view mirrors, some way in the distance. I was in the corner, which would take me around the inlet for maybe 600m, and I was holding good speed too, 85kph. The buzz on this huge corner was awesome.

Just as I started to come out of the second half of the corner I had the shock of my life as a German-registered BMW with pillion passenger overtook me, the rider almost kissing my boots to my left-hand side, and with his wheels almost touching the white lines to the centre of the road. Jesus, did I have a wake-up call! It panicked me a little and I eased off the gas slightly to right the bike a little and take another look in the mirrors. Two more to come, but they were in no hurry, so I took a breath and carried on.

As I exited the corner we were back on to dual carriageway. I could see the BMW way in the distance. Jesus that guy can ride, but whether he should have taken me at that specific point is something I think only he and I would ever be able to argue over. His mates, also German, waited until the road opened up, then let loose a solitary index finger, pointing up off the throttle hand as they passed me. I'm imagining I'm now one of their mates maybe, and I've been accepted as one of the boys. I will never know, as we didn't see them again. Bloody Germans!

It was Andorra next. Dave had eased up for me to catch him and thought it very funny as I vented my frustration over the German overtaking me in the middle of a corner, and he two-up. All Dave could do was laugh at me and tell me, "Lose some weight Lard Arse, then the bike might go a bit quicker." Some friend he is.

Andorra had provided a great ride there, but it was just before noon when we arrived and we were in the chaotic town, with vehicles everywhere, just like being back in the city of London on a Friday afternoon. We pulled into a garage to refuel and had a coffee whilst we decided the route we would take. Dave said there was a tunnel up ahead, then we would be able to traverse back into France. From there we would head for the Spanish border sometime after.

We set off and were only five minutes on the road when there was a huge sign for a toll ahead. Dave shouted over the intercom, "There is a sign to the right saying in English 'No toll road', do you fancy it?" Silly question really, and we headed for the no toll sign. We were back alone and almost immediately climbing very steeply, and like a game of snakes and ladders, we were easing up the side of this valley at some speed. The smile was back on my face and my misfortunes of the previous hour were behind me. We were soon at the top of the road and stopped to take in the views and understand where we were.

We were at the Encamp les Bon, on the CG-2, which was a road to dream of, and having taken in the views of the valley below looking back down into Andorra, we headed over the brow to carry on with our journey. That lasted all of about two minutes though, as just over the brow we were greeted by even more stunning views of the journey down into France and the road meandering away into the distance. This really was about to be a great ride down on what looked like a demanding road.

You can guess what came next, yes it was Dave time, and off he went again. I too was having a great ride, my confidence was high, we were on wide roads, and most of the time we had an overtaking lane too. The corners were large and very long, and it was like I was once again a part of the bike for the short while the journey took us down that road. This was the second time that I could say I really did feel that I was part of the machine that was underneath me. It lasted 11km and Dave was at the end of it with a large cheesy smile and already taking a few pictures of me as I approached him. What a great finish to the Pyrenees. It had been a part of the journey that I will never forget.

We were heading for the town of Puigcerdà, just inside the Spanish border and heading then for the town of Cardona. Riding out of France on the N-20 it was only twenty minutes before we were back into Spain and travelling south-east on the N-260 once again. We were on main roads but now slightly deflated as we knew the mountain section of our journey was almost at an end, so we had decided to stay with the faster roads for an hour or two to make good headway.

Just south of the town of Ripoll, we took a left turn and were now heading due west along the C-26. This road for the next hour gave us both some great fun. We were surrounded by the small foothills from the mountains we had just conquered, and were ascending and descending these smaller brothers and sisters like true professionals, and once again we had all the road to ourselves. We might have been a little sad to be leaving the Pyrenees but we had so much more fun ahead of us yet. We carried on along the C-26 until we arrived at the town of Berga, and from there we decided we would head overland on the smaller roads to find the town of Cardona, where we would stop and have a drink and rest for an hour whilst we decided where to stay tonight.

Being on the back roads was like coming home to an old friend. It's strange, but even after two weeks of riding it seemed to me that I was so much better on these tight corners with little room around me. We did have a completely different landscape around us too; behind us were the heavenly tops of the mountains and ahead were open fields and small farms scattered everywhere. Within an hour we were pulling into Cardona, a town in Catalonia, and in the province of

Barcelona. By now we were only 90km to the west of Barcelona, so the coastline was now within reach once again.

Cardona sits on a hill, almost completely surrounded by the river Cardener, and most definitely dominated by the Castle of Cardona. Although some of this huge castle dates back over twelve hundred years, the majority of it was rebuilt in the late 1700s and is arguably the most important medieval fortress in Catalonia, and one of the most important in Spain. I really must visit the town to a view the castle with Vanessa one day.

We found a small car park and parked the bikes, then walked through a large opening into the town square. There was some sort of a concert or occasion about to happen, as filling the square was purpose-made seating. It was almost as if they were about to shoot some of the action from the film *Gladiator*. As we walked into the centre of this newly built arena we saw what can only be described as the largest of all the Catalonian flags we had seen to date. Having seen hundreds in the past few days, this monster flag was at six storeys high, an estimated 20m high and approximately 10m wide. Everywhere you looked there were yellow ribbons attached to whatever could be found to attach them to. Smaller Catalonian flags were attached to every other window of all the buildings surrounding the square. This was like the central point of the whole independence of Catalonia. I might be wrong but these guys from Cardona don't class themselves as Spanish.

We walked through to the other side of the square and looked out directly at the castle in front of us. It was an awesome sight but at 2.30pm we did not have the time to take a look inside, so I will have to return for that another day. Coffee was a two-minute walk away, as well as some cold water, as we were now inland and at a lot lower altitude, so the temperature had risen considerably. The sweat was pouring out of me now, and it was about 29°C and getting hotter.

We looked at our options for hotels for the night and Dave found a nice place just over an hour and a half away in the town of Valls, just above Tarragona. The rest of our journey was to be via the main C-55 and then on to the road to Valls, the C-37. We wouldn't be distracted by main roads though, as we were in the middle of no-man's-land here in this corner of Spain. It was a lovely ride and the land was now no longer green but becoming very arid and scorched. We had a leisurely ride down and pulled into a quite new hotel just off the main drag before the town of Valles. The best thing was it had a bar and restaurant in the place and the rooms were fantastic.

We checked in and were on the ground floor, although we did have three steps to walk up to our floor. The room was large and clean. It was time to get the intercoms on charge, then chill for an hour. It was approaching 4.30pm now and the restaurant didn't open until 7pm, so I could catch up on writing my journal and take a shower. I even had a snooze for thirty minutes as I was knackered.

We headed down at 6.30pm to get a beer before the restaurant opened. We had San Miguel on draft, nice and cold, just what we needed. We were offered the menu and both went for pork steak and chips, not very adventurous but we had been eating all sorts the past few days with the rich tapas meals and we both just fancied plain and simple tonight. By 9pm, we had finished dinner, even had three beers, and we were both really tired. Even at such an early hour us two old boys knew where we were off to now – bed and a well-earned sleep.

Chapter 19

The Mediterranean Highway South En Route to Spain's Best Campsite (Really!)

Saturday, 29 September

31°C – clear blue skies

338km travelled today

We were up and all packed by 8am. Being so close to the coast now we had plans to hit the Mediterranean coastline and search for coffee and something to eat to set us up for the day. Our only other thing on the list of visits for this part of the journey was the Ebro Delta.

As we left the car park, which sat in shade, it felt rather cool. The sun was out and the skies were clear, but as we pulled out into the sunshine from the car park the temperature rose up from 12°C to what was a nice 23°C. Tarragona was our main target, towards the coast then pick up the N-340 and find a place to stop for breakfast.

We stopped on the seafront at La Pineda, and we had only been on the go for forty-five minutes. It was very warm, considerably warmer than our past few days in the Pyrenees. This seaside beach town is wedged between the towns of Tarragona and the party town of Salou, both of which I'm sure you will find in all the major tourist destination books for all the good and bad reasons. We pulled up a chair at the first café on the seafront, where a large sign outside said, 'Spain's best full English'. We were tempted but passed on such a huge start to the day, and settled for toast and a coffee.

It took only a few minutes and we sat and enjoyed breakfast whilst watching some of Europe's finest specimens start their sunny holidays in their shorts and T-shirts, regardless of their body size. We were looking at little and large one moment, waddling along the seafront, closely followed by Mrs Bucket giving strong orders to her following wimp of a husband. There were all nationalities strolling about at this early hour and all with the thought of eating, then hitting the beach. If nothing else, we did stand out as the oddest of all the people as we sat there in mid-twenty degree temperatures in full motorcycle gear, sweating in the morning sun.

Discussing the order of our day's adventure, we were once again in no rush. The Ebro Delta was only one and half hours away at a slow pace, so that was our mid-morning coffee destination, then back on to the highway southward bound. If either of us wanted to pull over to view something or take a picture, we just had to shout over the intercom or we could pull over.

Getting back to the N-340 was not as simple as getting off it, as we had a detour to contend with that lasted some twenty minutes, following diversion signs that were taking us round and round in circles. In the end we got fed up with the signs and rode a short section down a road that was having its surface renewed, albeit not today, as it was Saturday and everything in this closed-off road was deserted. A few minutes on and we re-joined the correct road, both a little peed-off about the signs. Maybe someone had had one beer too many last night and thought it a good idea to wind up some unsuspecting tourists on a Saturday morning by sending them round in circles until they cracked, or maybe me and Fat Man didn't read the signs correctly, both are definitely possible.

Only a short time later Dave called over the intercom that we needed to pull over as a management light had lit up on his bike and he wanted to check what it was. It turned out to be something and nothing. He turned his ignition off and looked up what the light was for, then when he turned the ignition back on the warning light had disappeared, never to come back on. I'm still not sure he told me what the fault was, but we moved on.

For the next hour or so on the way down to the delta, every time Dave pulled up to traffic lights or was in slow traffic, he stalled the bike. You can imagine I was having some fun winding him up as it was rather embarrassing seeing my riding partner stall his bike every time he pulled up. Dave, however, wasn't seeing the funny side of the matter. We weren't falling out but for a short while on that morning I could sense something had changed in both our moods. I let it be after a short while and we were now pulling off the main road at L'Ampolla and heading on to the delta. It is one of the largest wetland areas in the western Mediterranean. Huge areas of the delta have been drained for agricultural use over the years, with rice being the bulk of the crops grown there. If you ever visit the area, which is very beautiful, I'm sure like us, you will think you could be anywhere in Vietnam, there are so many rice fields.

We stopped a couple of times as we toured the region, first to view a huge flock of birds. I could not tell you what they were, but there were thousands of them flying high, then settling again for a few moments before it all started again.

Then they were up and off for a quick flight to settle their nerves, finishing up right back where they had started from only minutes before.

Our second stop was for our mid-morning coffee. Parking up right in the small high street of El Cave, we sat down at a tiny local bar. It was 11.30am now and the temperature was up to 31°C, so we sat in some shade that was offered by the small umbrella over the table. It was coffee and two cokes today, time to push the boat out. The guy serving us was in his mid-fifties, if I was to guess, not too many teeth either, and his clothes were in need of at least a wash if not replacing. He was a pleasant enough guy though.

At the next table was a very elderly chap, perhaps late seventies, smoking his filterless cigarettes and sipping his coffee and brandy. He was being tormented by a young man who really didn't seem to have all the sandwiches packed in his picnic; well if they were all there, some were missing the filling shall we say. Let's call him Selwyn just to give him a name. In his hands he was holding a pigeon. I'm not sure whether it was alive or not but Selwyn kept walking up to the old guy and pushing the pigeon under his nose.

This happened several times, with the old man politely waving him away. Then Selwyn shot into the bar and started running around with the bird still in his hands, so the guy who had served us chased him outside. At that time both Dave and I actually thought we were going to be dragged into this fiasco. Selwyn, though, clutched his bird close to his chest and shouted a few Spanish obscenities before just walking off down the road. Well, that is after poking it for one last time under the nose of the old guy at the next table. Everything went back to normal and we ordered another coffee. The guy serving us smiled and made a motion of crazy man with his right hand and we drank our coffees.

We discussed where we would stay tonight. Now we were back in the warmer climates we agreed we would take a night's camping, but Dave was adamant we were not going to be drinking port. He was sure his tent would hold out for one night after the damage inflicted during our last camping stop.

Setting off, we rode behind a rice tractor for several miles before he headed off into the fields and we could exit the delta. As we approached the turning back on to the N-340, we rode over a large bridge spanning the river Ebro, the same river we had been fishing on several months earlier in the year. The bridge was covered in the yellow ribbons once again, so we were still in Catalonia then.

We were keeping a good speed but the coast was not always in our sights. I knew this road only too well, having travelled it for several years every summer with our touring caravan and now to visit our twin sons, who live just outside Marbella. We were not enjoying the day's ride though, and I felt there was something we were missing. It came to me as we rode away from the Ebro – I think we were both starting to feel a little homesick. I could not discuss it with Dave whilst we were riding but I would broach the subject at some time today.

The next couple of hours passed by with nothing really to get excited about. We were travelling on a good single carriageway road with little traffic on it, and occasionally it would open up into dual carriageway and we could let our bikes open up a little. Several times during that stint we hit the magic 160kph (100mph). I'm starting to get a bit blasé about it too.

It was approaching 1.30pm and to our right the coast was about a kilometre or more away. We passed a sign for the coastal town of Peñíscola, and Dave said he had been to a town with the very same name in the USA a year or two ago, so he would like to pop in and have a look. No problem, as it was coffee time once again. We entered the town on the same road we would later leave on. It was a lovely seaside town, deep beach with glorious golden sand, and lots of it. To the right as we pulled up on the seafront was a large castle dominating the skyline looking over the town. The beach has a huge promenade running all the way along it and there is quite a stretch to take a good walk if you want. We, however, settled for a couple of pictures at the edge of the beach, then crossed the road to find a café to have a drink.

The place was heaving. There were small cafés everywhere and it took several minutes before we spotted one small enough to get served quickly but with an empty table. We could also see the bikes from where we sat, which was an added bonus. It was coffee and coke again, really pushing the boat out, and definitely no expense spared on our drinking today. The waiter serving us asked where we were from and whether we were on bikes. That's a simple observation, with the gear we were wearing and helmets in hand. "Yes," we replied.

Then he pointed to our two bikes, "Are they yours?" he asked in Spanish. We explained as best we could about our journey so far and our final destination. He spoke no English so the Spanglish and hand signals were in full flow once again. He too was a biker, and he loved to ride his bike every Sunday, but not in the summer months as there were too many crazy people on holidays. We all had a good chuckle. It was nice how people just wanted to chat about what we were doing on this journey.

I asked Dave if he was okay, and I explained I was feeling a little down today, probably as we were not hanging off the mountains as we had been the past few days. He too was a bit fed up, and it all seemed a little false now that we had travelled so far and experienced so much. Yet we were now on quite mundane roads with little excitement in them. I couldn't disagree and suggested we thought about cutting the trip back a few days. It was now Saturday, and riding slowly we could be back in Marbella by Tuesday.

The coast road here was not like the southern or northern regions of Spain, or even Portugal for that matter. We were not able to hug the majority of the coast, as there were so many holiday beach towns running along the coastline. Dave said he would think it over, and I ordered another coffee. By the time the coffee was on the table Dave had new ferry dates on screen and we discussed just what timescale we could achieve without damaging the whole journey we had set out to do.

It was a three-day ride back from here realistically, with some good areas of coast road too. We were only 650km from the finish line, and with another seven days set aside to do it in. We would realistically be travelling at the same speed and covering the same mileage daily anyway if we made Marbella by Tuesday. Dave called his ferry company to see if he was able to change his crossing from Santander to Portsmouth to bring it forward to the Thursday evening. It was only a five-minute call, and he had a new ferry booked, although he had to pay a small charge, as they only had a suite cabin available. We were both now committed to a three-day ride home to Marbella, beginning tomorrow, and not the seven days of our original plan. A huge weight had been lifted from my shoulders and I think Dave felt just the same. I know what you're thinking – we're both a couple of old softies, but in answer to that all I can say is yes, you're right.

Before we knew it we were back on the road and, as I said earlier, heading back out the same way we came in. We had a buzz about us again. We weren't chasing tight-cornered twisties now, or the lure of the mountains, it was the finish line, and on a timescale. Most importantly, the light at the end of this ride was there in the distance and starting to grow bigger now.

We were now looking for our destination just before Valencia, a campsite Dave said had some of the best reviews on his satnav app. We headed south and before too long we were riding alongside the toll road, the AP-7, which was to be our chaperone for the best part of an hour. The scenery was quite drab after what we had been used to, but to our right and looking inland we had a mountain range that would be our companion for the whole journey home now, and at times we would be seeking some adventure in those mountains too.

The further south we rode the more burnt and arid the scenery became. Even the mountain ranges were starting to take on a sandy look, as though they too had been burnt over generations of fierce sunshine, bleaching their colour away. It was now that one of Dave's famous sayings would keep getting blurted down my intercom, "Look at the mountains over there Lard Arse; just how lucky are we?" In fairness, he was spot on, we were very lucky at such a young age to be exploring as we were.

But it was time for me to join in with the drivel and come up with one of my own sayings in rebuff, "It is what it is Fat Man".

An hour later we were looking up to our left and the dominating castle on the skyline that looked down on to the coastal town of Castellón de la Plana. This huge castle was once a walled city and almost impenetrable. It wasn't until the 19th century that the walls were removed from the outreaches of the castle and the town started to grow until it is what we see today. These days its most famous son is Sergio Garcia the Spanish professional golfer. We had no time to stop, as it would need a day to visit this town, so it's now on my to-visit list, as we headed on for another thirty minutes.

We were now heading for the campsite, just off the coast and approximately 30km south of Castellón de la Plana, at a small seaside village called Moncofa. Only ten minutes after passing the castle, Dave's intercom stopped working. Yes, he had forgot to charge it last night; muppet, or was he fed up with me singing 'Sweet Soul Music' into his ears? He then turned off the main road and started to ride down a dirt track alongside the road, turning into a large olive grove. We managed to encircle the whole grove and come right back to where we entered it before Dave pulled over to tell me his satnav was having a mad moment. I suggested he turn the thing off and reset the route as these things happen sometimes. Then we did have a problem. His satnav was telling us we needed to catch a ferry to Ibiza and then another one to Valencia. Great start, or should I say finish to this day.

He cancelled the route and we headed towards the road once again, trying to retrace our steps. We weren't able to communicate due to his dead intercom, but Dave all of a sudden was on a mission. His satnav must have come back to life, as he waved his left arm in a circular motion above his head, urging us to turn around, and we were off again, back into the olive grove but this time going in the opposite direction. Next it was under a road bridge that really was a tight squeeze it was so low, then out into an orange orchard, closely followed by an almond grove. If only his intercom was working I could have really given him some earache. You need to remember that each of these orchards was a good five to six minutes to ride through as they were huge.

Finally we hit tarmac and there was a fuel station ahead. I pulled up alongside Dave and told him to stop in there as I needed fuel. As I refuelled, Dave could see the campsite on his satnav map, and we were 300m away. Back on the hunt, we found the site with little trouble and pulled into what I can only describe as a dump. Removing my helmet I asked Dave if this was the right place, which he said it was. It was cheap and there was lots of room too.

We checked in and were shown to a field where we were to set the tents. The ground was covered with small stones, not grass, so we had to choose the right pitch or we would be in for a rough night. Half an hour later, at 6pm, we were all set up. Tents were made and Dave's tent was just about standing, even though it was a little, shall we say, 'on the Huh', one of those good old Suffolk sayings.

Time to go and find some food, as once again we hadn't eaten since breakfast way back in La Pineda this morning. We headed towards the sea, as it was only a two-minute walk, where there were several bars but none serving food. We walked a good mile along the promenade before turning around, slightly peeved, as we could not find anything. On the way back, just before the campsite, there was a bit of a posh restaurant or bar opening up. We asked if they were serving food and they said not until 7pm, but we could sit and enjoy a beer if we wished.

It was not the warmest of evenings, even though it had been up to 31°C during the day. The wind was blowing hard now and at a guess it was in the mid-teens temperature-wise. Anyway, we enjoyed a couple of beers and chatted about our newly made plans, and agreed that, in hindsight, maybe we should have taken a few more days exploring the Pyrenees. It was agreed in the end, though, that we had had a fantastic time and we really didn't have any regrets. We would both end up home in our own beds three or even four days earlier, and back with our beloved wives (that's another Brownie point for me in Vanessa's eye).

The menu card was out and nothing really appealed to either of us. Dave plumped for a fish dish and I went for a cured meat platter, neither of which were too much to write home about. Heading back after our expensive evening meal and beers we decided to have a couple in the campsite bar, as it was Saturday night after all. There was no draft beer, it was all bottled, and we were on the Estrella again. We only had a couple, as the night fell dark and we were both hanging once again. Riding several thousand kilometres really does take its toll on you. It was bed and shuteye now, in Dave's best campsite.

Chapter 20

It's a Madge Mobile Race then on to the Land of Submarines

Sunday, 30 September

29°C – clear blue skies with light cloud

356km travelled today

I slept like an absolute log overnight, more than could be said for the Fat Man next to me, who was showered, dressed and starting to pack his tent already as I crawled out of my tent. Strange how being on your own and not sharing a room makes you sleep so well. Anyway, I headed off for a shower and tidy up before heading back and packing all my kit away. This would be our last time camping, as we had another two nights to go in hotels, and we had already decided they would be the best hotels we could find, within reason for us two tight old gits.

I collected our rubbish, having both cleaned our helmet visors, and headed to find a bin. On my way back to the bikes a Spanish guy appeared from his touring caravan and started to enquire were we were from and ask about our journey. Once again I was thrown into my Spanglish and arm waving to get to what I wanted to say to him, but it didn't matter, the guy loved what we were doing and was all smiles and happy for the two of us. Soon we were shaking hands, then Dave and I were mounting up and heading out.

We exited the campsite and it wasn't a moment too soon. The place was a dump, not the best in the area as Dave had informed me. The intercoms were working again, as Dave had remembered to charge his, and I was having a little dig at him about the fact that in his opinion what was the best campsite was very clearly over exaggerated. We were only 400m down the road when on our right-hand side, right next to the campsite we had been in was the campsite we were supposed to have stay at. Yes, it had a huge bar and restaurant, big shop and three swimming pools. It looked almost new, not almost dead like the one we had been in. You can imagine I was giving Dave a real hard time now, and his bloody crazy satnav.

Talking of Dave's satnav, the morning had not been too good either for the poorly thing. We had put the name of El Palmar in, a small town en route on the coast road to the south side of Valencia. Problem was, once again, his satnav wanted to return to Barcelona and take a ferry to Ibiza and then a ferry back to Valencia. You can imagine why Dave was getting so much stick from me, but all good fun though. It was Google Maps to the rescue, as we planned our route and Dave noted the junctions down on a piece of paper, placing it in the top of his tank bag on display so he could read it whilst riding.

We travelled around Valencia with no mishaps. The place is huge. I visited it a few years back with Vanessa and the city itself is a lovely place to be, but it can be very hot! It was in the forties in mid-August when we were previously there and quite oppressive. This time we travelled the short distance down the coast road, through El Palmar, then through to Les Palmeres, staying all the time on a small road, the CV-500. This led into the town of Sueca, and it was time for a coffee and something to eat.

Breakfast was memorable for all the wrong reasons. We found two cafés next to each other; one was packed and had no seats available, and the second had only two young guys eating and chatting away, with endless seating available. So it was café number two we headed for, parking up, then sitting down in the morning sunshine, hanging our jackets on the chairs. We waited over ten minutes for a young Indian man to come and serve us. True to form I used my limited Spanish.

Rightly or wrongly I love to try to speak in the native language. I think it shows I'm trying to integrate and not rely on the age old "Do you speak English mate?" I'm actually fluent in German, having lived in either Germany of Austria for over fifteen years out of the past twenty-five, so being able to communicate with the locals is something I love doing. Today, however, this young guy was not having it. I think maybe he had the hump because it was early on a Sunday morning. Maybe he had been on a promise the night before and had to walk away because of an early shift. Either way, every time I spoke he would grunt back in English, which is something that really does get my goat. If I've taken time to speak your language, my attitude is at least respect me and answer back in Spanish, regardless of whether I understand it or not.

Eventually we ordered, and Dave thought it highly amusing that I was getting annoyed with the young man and started sledging me over it. Breakfast came, two cheese toasties. We had ordered coffee too but it came ten minutes later, and most definitely the worst coffee we had had all journey. I really was not happy now and asked for the bill. Twenty minutes later the bill still had not arrived, so I went inside to pay. Using no

Spanish I asked the middle-aged Indian lady behind the counter for my bill. She replied to me in perfect English that it was €12. She asked if everything was okay and whether we had enjoyed our breakfast, and my answer was that we certainly had with the exception of 'Kevin' the grumpy teenager who had served us.

I know Vanessa would have given me grief for saying this to the lady had she been with me, but she wasn't. I then went on to say that he was in need of some good manners, which should have been taught by his parents. She immediately replied that she was the young man's mother, so I picked up my change from the counter, looked at her and said, "I rest my case", and left the café. It took me a short while to calm down and Dave wasn't helping either, by rubbing me up over it for the next half hour.

Whilst I had been inside paying for breakfast, Dave had gone through the 'reset all' functions on the satnav, as I had suggested to him. For an engineer, Dave's common sense does need some working on, and I had told him that a few times on this journey too. By some miracle the satnav was back in business and showing a good route to our destination of the day, Cartagena, via a stop-off in the famous Benidorm for dinner.

Travelling now on our road of the day, the N-332, we were not exactly inland but the coast was some distance away too. We had decided to try to keep with the main N-332, then on to the N-340 to ensure we made good time now that we had our new end-date to be in Marbella by Tuesday morning. This would enable Dave to have a good rest before heading off early Wednesday to get back to Bilbao for Thursday afternoon, and his ferry back to the UK that night.

For the next hour and a half we were following the sea a kilometre or two away to our left and the mountain range that was always travelling with us to our right. We discussed over the intercoms how Spain is famous for sea, sun and sand but I've never heard of anyone saying they're going to Spain to go mountain walking or hiking. The mountains really were some range too, and they were to be with us all the way down to Marbella.

Dave was feeling much better, as was I, after we had agreed to head back a little earlier to complete the journey. He even told me that it was a huge surprise to him that we had not seen as many of the 'UK's finest' whilst stopping in the past two days on our journey. He had thought that the whole east coast would be tacky and full of marauding Brits having their meat pies and pint of UK bitter. I must admit that was also my first perception several years back, before Vanessa and I started exploring the country of Spain, and although it does have its seedy places, on the whole it has so much to explore and enjoy. That's why we keep coming back.

Getting on for 1pm and we were coming up to Benidorm. If you have never been it's a real must-visit town, even if only for a couple of hours as in our case. The skyline was dominated by a huge rock jutting into the sky as we approached Benidorm, which was the town of Calp. The rock looked like it was right in the middle of the seaside town, right on the coast. Approaching Benidorm ten minutes later we headed into the old town and towards the old marina, where it was busy, very busy, as we were riding down the small streets and through tight corners.

When we got to the beach area to the right of the marina, we could see there was some kind of festival happening, as everyone was in fancy dress and there were stalls selling everything from beer and tapas to cheap souvenirs for your holiday presents. I told Dave to take his next right-hand turning, as I knew a little of the area, having visited it a couple of times before. We were heading back out of the old town, so I told Dave to pull over. We had a quick chat and decided to head for the new side of town, the one made famous by the TV series with the same name, *Benidorm*.

It's only a three-kilometre ride to get to the other side, or new town, and when we reached it, we parked the bikes in a small side road and headed along the seafront for a walk on the promenade. Again Dave was very surprised at how nice the place was compared to what he had imagined it to be. I told him he needed to spend a few days here and he would soon realise why it has such a reputation for being a crazy town.

With the heat of the day, neither of us was hungry, but both very thirsty, so we sat down in a seafront café and ordered two sparkling waters and a coffee each. That's when Dave got a glimpse of just why you have to love Benidorm. From our right as we looked out to the beach, a young lady was speeding down the main beachfront promenade at all of 10kph. She had a white veil on her head that was trailing behind her due to the extreme speed she was travelling at. She was also wearing a short, very short, white skirt that just about covered up the bits that needed covering up, well at least until she cocked her leg over the saddle to exit the mobility scooter, or Madge mobile as I call them, that she was riding.

Dave looked at me and we both started to chuckle. I was just about to say, "That's why we came to Benidorm", when about 100m behind the bride-to-be came the hen party, all wearing pink veils and matching pink skirts. By the look of them they were the best part of gone with the wind already and it was only 2pm. We both laughed and it was another memory to place against the journey we were on.

We were just discussing the crazy place when no more than two minutes after the ladies had gone by, a guy came past with a white dickie bow around his neck and a white top hat on his head. We couldn't make out whether he was wearing anything else, but on seeing his entourage, who were hard on his heels, they were in black dickie bows and black top hats with small black thongs on. Absolute carnage going on and they were all out to have fun, not realising they were bringing fun to all who could see them too. What an afternoon we were having. We ordered another drink before heading on towards the Alicante area and the town of Torrevieja.

Dave's parents had spent the best part of twenty-five years since they had retired visiting this area of Spain for the winter months, as many Brits do. Dave was quite familiar with the region as we headed south, as he had visited his parents several times with Caroline. I too was no newcomer to the region, having stayed a few years back just outside Torrevieja for a week with my old touring caravan. Today it was the most traffic we had seen for days, if not our whole journey, as we rode around the region of Alicante.

It was another thirty minutes on and we were looking for fuel. It was almost 4pm and I suggested to Dave that we get a cold drink too as it was extremely hot. Dave pulled into a petrol station and, as we fuelled up, he suggested we take a short detour, only five minutes, to the campsite where his mum and dad used to camp each year. Just before the campsite we pulled over, parked the bikes on the road, headed into a lovely little bar and ordered cold drinks. Dave gave his dad a quick call and sent him a couple of pictures of the two of us in the bar. His dad didn't answer the call but I'm sure he enjoyed seeing Dave on his old stomping ground.

Dave found and booked us a nice hotel in the seaside town of Cartagena, which is only about an hour from where we were having a drink. He found a great place, with four stars, just a little way outside of town, including parking, and very cheap. We were all booked in to the place now, so it was time to hit the road for the last time today and see what this evening had to offer us.

We could not find the car park when we got to the hotel, so we parked on the road outside and entered reception to ask where to park. The lovely friendly young lady said she would let us into the parking area once we had checked in, which we did, then parked the bikes in the hotel's safe parking area. It had a 10ft fence around it, under one of those Spanish covered parking roof areas, not that the sun was going to be too strong overnight.

Before we headed up to our room the young receptionist asked if we were here to visit the carnival. We asked her to explain, and it turned out we were here on the last night of a nine-day festival to celebrate the Carthaginian and Roman legions. I can't go into too much detail, other than she explained they had been fighting and displaying their moves for the past eight days, as well as all sorts of activities, including Carthaginian bingo, dance fairs and druid sacrifices, all concluding today with the 'day of the bloody on your hands'. Not forgetting the huge fun fair that was on until 2am in the morning. The receptionist said all her girlfriends would be there until the morning having many drinks and enjoying the last night, whilst she worked the late shift, poor girl.

It all sounded interesting but not interesting enough to get us two old farts to go, especially as there was an entrance fee too. No, we were going to shower, walk down to the port area, see what sights Cartagena had to offer, then take a walk through town to find a nice place to eat, possibly even find a bar for a drink on the way back, as the hotel bar was shut tonight. The staff in the hotel bar were all probably drinking beer at the carnival tonight, so maybe that's why it was shut.

By 6pm we were ready to go out. Dave suggested we have a burger night as we had not had one so far on the trip. I had no problem with that, but please not McDonald's. Dave agreed, we could walk into town, look around the port and then through the town. On our way back to the hotel was a Burger King, or we could do it the other way round and eat first. Sounded like Dave had it all planned out. I suggested we eat first, then we could walk the burger off.

We were in the back roads making our way towards Burger King, which was only 700m away from the hotel, and we passed a couple of local bars, real local bars, the ones that holidaymakers would definitely not pop into for a beer. We made a mental note, as they were only three minutes from the hotel on the way home. The Burger King looked closed when we found it, but we tried the door, which opened, but there was no one in the place. We looked over the menu and both decided on the double whopper with bacon and cheese, not forgetting diet coke and a large side of chips. Cholesterol overload tonight.

It was made to order so we picked up our drinks and sat down watching the people walking around outside the place. It was nice to get a real cold coke and chill out this early in the evening. We both had a chuckle over the motorised mobility scooters in Benidorm and once again we had a memory that would stay with us forever. Dinner can only be described as huge, hardly a culinary masterpiece, but it was a big pile of stodge, which ticked all the boxes this evening. We took a refill on the drinks and headed off in search of the port.

Cartagena is not only famous for being a huge Roman city in its heyday in years long forgotten, but it is one of Spain's largest naval bases and houses the Spanish Navy's Maritime Department of the Mediterranean. Today the wind was blowing very hard, and there was a very cold breeze over the whole port area, so we only took a short walk around it and headed for warmer climes and through the town area. The town has some lovely architecture and we strolled through it, taking a few pictures before the sun disappeared. As we slowly walked back towards the hotel, we came across a building that was unmistakably from the architect Gaudi and turned out to be a public building in this town, on the left of the main street as we headed up it.

We came across a large roundabout paying tribute to the naval presence, with a miniature-sized submarine placed right in the middle of it. We walked back past Burger King, where we had eaten only a little over an hour ago, then it was on the look-out for one of the bars we had seen earlier. It was just after 8pm, we were both hanging, tired and still full from the burger we had eaten earlier.

The first of the bars was closed as we walked past but the second bar, which was only 100m further on, was still open and had three locals at the bar watching a football game on the TV and drinking beer. We ordered two small beers and sat watching the football, just catching up on another eventful day once again. Tomorrow was to be our very last full day's travelling and we decided we would look to stay in the town of Motril, halfway between the towns of Almeria and Malaga. It would be only about a two-hour ride to Malaga from there and a little over three hours to Marbella, give or take a stop or two as well.

We only had the one beer in the bar, even though when we went out earlier we were discussing having two or three, but it just was not going down very well. The accumulation of a huge dinner and both of us being very tired was too much tonight. We finished our beers and headed back to chill out and get some well-earned sleep. Once again these two old gits were hanging and starting to show their age, as well as feeling it too. Yes,   old   …   very   old.

Chapter 21

Our One and Only 'Lady of the Day' and a Mini Hollywood Washout in the Desert

Monday, 1 October

29°C – cloudy with occasional thunder showers

349km travelled today

We woke and were dressed by 8am, ready to leave. As each day went by now we were getting very tired. Our planned day off every week had not happened, and after eighteen days non- stop there was no wonder it was catching up with us.

As we loaded our cases on to the bikes and headed out of the hotel car park we had one thing on our mind – it was churros for breakfast. We had spotted a small stall, well more like a cabin, opposite Burger King the night before. We had looked to see what time it opened, but there was nothing to tell us; however, it would be a great way to start our last full day if it was open.

Good news, it was open, but there was so much traffic and nowhere to park, so we circled the area twice and decided we would park on the pavement right next to the cabin and take our chances with any parking wardens that may appear. The smell was wonderful, and we grabbed a table inside the small tented area next to the cabin and I went up to order coffee and the churros. If you have never heard of or eaten churros before, they are made from a thick dough pastry mix, traditionally coming from Spain or Portugal, but these days they can be found throughout southern America too, as I'd eaten them in Lima some years ago.

In Spain, churros are a long thin stick of dough dropped into hot fat to be cooked. They are usually eaten for breakfast, dipped in hot chocolate, coffee or a bowl of sugar, and are often sprinkled with sugar on top too. You might want to eat them as we did today, with all of the above – coffee, sugar sprinkled over them and with a bowl of sugar, absolutely delicious and one of the best breakfast starts we had on the whole trip. Even better was that at €4 for the two of us it was a really cheap way to fill up and start the morning's ride.

Setting out now the skies looked like we were entering a wet drizzle ahead as we climbed out of the region on the E-22, a really small country lane that gave us some great fun, especially as it turned out to be a heavy sea mist, not rain, and the roads were dry. We stayed with the small road through to the village of Isla Plana, and for a short while we were right on the coast, with a quite wild sea battering the cliffs that we were riding along. Before too long we were on the RM-322 main drag and heading around the port of Mazarrón to carry on west along this main coastal road.

As the skies were slowly clearing of the mist we could see the jungle of polytunnels that the region of Almeria is famous for. This region of Spain's economy is built heavily around vegetable production, with hundreds of thousands of acres of greenhouses, which supply much of Europe, especially through the winter months, with fresh vegetables and fruit. It is, however, not a nice sight, as this kind of industrial production is quite a blight on the landscape.

By 11am the skies were clear and we were looking for a coffee just outside the seaside town of Marinas. We parked the bikes on the main road and sat down at a table in the late morning sun. Coffee was very nice and we discussed our trip to Tabernas, the region of Spain that was made famous in the 1960s for the Spaghetti westerns filmed in this Spanish desert region.

The film set of Fort Bravo, one of the original villages constructed for the film industry in this region, is situated by a canyon and is only accessible now by an adventurous ride through a dry valley, where you first ride past a border post, pay your entrance fee and park at the gates of the fort. From then on it's like you're looking for Clint Eastwood every minute of the day. You really have to rub your eyes when you're there to believe that you are here in Europe. The cacti, the vastness of the terrain, the sun-drenched light that bathes the scene, and the whole atmosphere of the film village makes the trip a memorable one. So that was our destination but we had to get there first.

Once again it was a break from the coastal route but it's our journey and we are the ones who make the rules on it. We headed off after our coffee and picked up a very small road, the A-370, towards Los Gallardos, from where we would then take the N-340a cross country to Tabernas to visit Fort Bravo. The roads were really good and once again very quiet. We got as far as Almocáizar, where we took a left out of town, staying with the N-340a. We had a few drops of rain starting to fall now and the skies did look to be darkening.

It was then that we saw our first and only 'Lady of the Day' on the whole journey. If you're unsure what these ladies are, they are usually dressed very scantly, with undersized short hot pants and bikini tops, normally sitting on a white plastic chair close to a main road and looking to generate trade from passing motorists. Yes, the oldest profession in the world is there on full view on many of Spain's busy countryside roads. We had been very lucky so far, and this was the only one we had seen, and it would turn out to be our last on the journey.

As we rode past this 'Lady of the Day', who was clad in bright purple hot pants and a bright orange bikini top, high heels, and was smoking away on a fag, I could not help but bib my horn and give her a wave. She smiled and waved back. Dave told me to stop being so childish, but I told him that it was a lucky sign to see a scantily clad lady, and maybe that meant we would have no rain today. "We will see," came back over the intercom. He can be such a grump.

We were now heading inland, and the ride was getting better. We were chasing our own tails and attacking the twisties yet again, moving into the hills and mountains of this region, and it was great fun for us. After so much time the week before in the Pyrenees I was taking this as my final test of steep and sharp corners, through this very deserted region with great riding roads. Most of all I was loving every minute of this last day.

We stopped several times for pictures and to view the deserted region. There were so many dwellings that had been abandoned and they just melted into the landscape so that it wasn't until you actually stopped to look closely that you could see them. There was a yellowy arid look to the whole region now and the deserted properties looked like they were built from either rock or a mud brick of the very same colour. Very few had any form of roof covering, leading us to think they had been this way for many a year.

By 1pm we had our first sighting of the motion picture industry in the desolate region. A huge sign, 'Texas Hollywood', was in the distance in huge white letters. We stopped and took a few pictures of this and the whole region. It was at this time that we could see what had been building up behind us as we were riding – a storm with sheet lightning was heading our way.

We jumped back on the bikes and made the short distance to the entrance to Fort Bravo, in the hope that the storm would be going in a different direction to us. No such luck. We pulled up on the opposite side of the fort entrance, but rain was starting to fall now. Not any old rain, it was very large spots and getting heavier. We had a choice to make and quickly – do we stay to visit the fort and hope it blows over soon or do we head off and try to outrun the storm in the hope we stayed dry.

We were running, and not a moment too soon. We had to turn in the direction of the storm first, and for ten minutes we were in torrential rain before the road moved away and we were then trying to stay ahead of the wet stuff. Wet and damp, we were back on dry roads within fifteen minutes, but we needed to move quickly to stay dry.

Travelling now on the A-348 we were still on the great twisty roads and managing to keep on dry roads. With no real time to pay too much attention to the surrounding region, our aim was stay dry and keep going. Another hour and we were away and it appeared we had beaten the storm so far. We came into the village of Cherín and pulled over right between two petrol stations at a small café. We were both buzzing after some of the best and quickest riding time we had had on the journey to beat the storm. I knew that at times in the past hour I really was on my limit of bike riding, and I was extremely happy to have survived in one piece whilst trying my best to keep to Dave's pace and not lose the bike at the same time.

We ordered coffee and sat down inside. The rain looked like it had caught up with us, but who cares, we were inside now and having a break. It was nothing but a passing shower thankfully, and within half an hour we were on the road again. Dave had booked our room for the night and it was another top four-star hotel, this time in Motril. It was after 3.30pm, we had over 170km to travel, and neither of us wanted to end up wet this close to our journey's end.

Staying with the A-348, we needed to travel west before we could get a road that would take us south in the direction of Motril. The roads were dry within ten minutes of our leaving the café, so it really was just a passing shower. The ride was just awesome and we were loving it, as well as having a little more time to enjoy it now as the skies had cleared. It was still dark but there was no thunder and lightning to be seen or heard now.

Neither of us had paid attention to our fuel situation, and we were supposed to fill up when we last stopped but both clearly forgot. Dave had a track on it though, and could see that ahead in the village of Cádiar there was a petrol station showing on the satnav. It was on our route, only about 15km away, and we had both got approximately 50km of fuel left.

We were saved as we entered this white village. Dave said there were two fuel stations, not one, the first of which we rode past, as it was closed and had been for several years. The second turned out to be a self-service card payment pump that looked like it had been installed back in the 1970s. It had no instructions and no computer screen to tell us how to use it. We were in need of fuel and it wasn't coming from this village, so we carried on riding.

I was following Dave as we exited the village, and his satnav had a little blip as we were trying to get back to the main A-348. It took us into the heart of the village. If we had stopped at any time through these village roads we would have been able to touch the walls of the buildings either side of the road. Cars would never have been down these roads before, just us two crazy Englishmen were stupid enough to do that!

Before long we came to an opening on the outskirts of the village, where there was a mini roundabout. We had a choice – take the very small road to our left that looked to lead into nowhere, go straight over the roundabout into the village again, or turn right on to what we believed was a shortcut back to the road on which we had just travelled into the village. Right it was then, and up a small cobbled road, quite steep, with a right turn 200m up it. It was then a short twisty section of about 50m, which was a dead end in front, or right down another small cobbled road, but we were not able to see where that one went.

We had no choice, unable to turn around and return the way we had come, due to the roads being so narrow. We had to turn right, then after another 50m we had to turn left, but now we were in trouble. We could see the roundabout just below us once again, but we had a 90-degree turn to make left then directly 180 degrees right on a road that was no wider than five feet. This was going to be a full-concentration manoeuvre to ensure neither of us dropped the bikes.

I went first. The left-hand turn was a slightly better corner, as the road was just that bit wider, but it was a three-point manoeuvre to position myself for the right hander and I was scraping the walls to my left as I held the bike on the front brake while leaning at 35 degrees to my right, also trying to reverse several times to give the room to get the front wheel around this corner. On several occasions I was over-revving the bike accidentally whilst keeping the brake full on.

By now the bike was getting heavier by the second, not the minute, and I was sure I couldn't hold it for too much longer. The sweat was pouring out of me. I also needed to raise my visor, as the heat coming off me was causing it to steam up inside. I stopped everything for a moment to take stock, and by this time an old man in his seventies was 50m in front of me shouting at me in Spanish. I had no idea what he was saying but by his body language I assume he was telling us that we were complete idiots for riding through his village and down his small narrow street on our bikes.

I made my last manoeuvre forward and this time managed to get the front wheel around past the wall and ride down the road by the roundabout. All through this Dave had been telling me calmly to take my time, but if I dropped it I'd be on my own, as he wouldn't be able to help as he needed to keep hold of his bike. On parking my bike I immediately told Dave to wait there. I kept my helmet on so we could communicate and was running back up the street past my new best friend the Spanish guy and telling Dave to wait for me. After all, his bike was much heavier than mine and if I could help I would. He had made it though; as I passed the old guy, Dave eased past the wall to his left and his front wheel was into open road, albeit a very small narrow cobbled one.

A lady appeared now and was talking to the old Spanish guy. I could make out that she was telling him we were stupid foreigners and not to waste his breath talking to us. What can you say to that? I apologised to both the lady and man in English and mounted up. We followed the road up the small lane that we should have taken on the left of the roundabout, and within 300m we were back on the A-348 main route out of the village. I was behind Dave once again and at that time I'm sure we were both confident about the fuel situation, as we still had over twenty miles of fuel each in the tanks.

We kept climbing and were enjoying the beautiful twisty roads, even though we were now on some very small mountain passes heading south on the A-345 towards the village of Morones, and still no petrol station. After passing through this village it was a right on to the GR-5202, an even smaller mountain road than the A-345. We were climbing again, but only for about 8km, and slowly. Finally we plateaued out and it was spitting with rain once again, as the storm was back with us.

We could see for miles all around us, but we were both now down to our last 16km of fuel. Dave looked on the satnav, which said there was a Repsol garage 24km away. We discussed and agreed over the intercoms that Dave would go on as quickly as he dared, as it now looked mostly downhill, and he was to search for fuel and hopefully make it to the garage. I was going to carry on by myself as I had two fewer kilometres showing on my indicator, so it would be better if I just cruised down with no throttle as long as possible and ride it out for as much as I could.

Dave was only in range on the intercom for a short while and I was then on my own. The worst part about this situation was that we were riding some of the best roads we had seen all day. Okay, they were not wide and we were really in the middle of nowhere but you could see 400–500m ahead, even with so many corners

We were descending quickly now and now Dave was out of sight too. I kept going and it took almost fifteen minutes before the fuel gauge was reading zero. By this time I could see a main road about a kilometre below me to my left as I descended into a large wide valley. I could just make out a motorbike on the dual carriageway below me, riding away to my left. I was hoping that was Dave. I kept going, then when I came to the bottom of my descent I had a choice to make, left or right. I presumed it was Dave I had seen earlier so that meant left and hope for the best.

I hit the main road, dreading that my bike would stop at any moment, but it kept going. I was now 6km down the dual carriageway and I could see in the distance a Repsol garage. I opened up the throttle, as I was only about a kilometre away, thinking I could open up the bike and if the fuel ran out at speed I could then cruise into the petrol station.

Dave had made it and was filling up his bike as I cruised in. We greeted each other with huge smiles and sighs of relief. I filled up and bought a couple of chocolate bars and a coffee each, then we just sat to eat and drink, relieved about averting our possible disaster today. When we looked at our odometers, we had travelled, over 80km since we first realised we were down to a 50km range. We had been extremely lucky, and managed to stay dry up until now, with the exception of a couple of small showers.

It was a dash for Motril now and we had just over 80km to go. Leaving the petrol station, we headed back south to pick up the main N-340a, then west to Motril, our hotel and our last night out before our arrival back at Marbella, having completed a circumference of the Iberian peninsula. Once we merged on to the main road west, we both opened the bikes up and it was a relief not to have to look at the fuel gauges. It was time to get to our hotel as soon as possible. Mind you, on entering Motril, Dave's satnav did have a little wobble once again and took us to the port area, which required a short boat trip then across the small bay at Motril to get to the hotel the other side. It was all we needed after a long day. After a quick turnaround and the use our noses to get on to the beach road, we then discovered we were in a very posh and classy hotel.

We checked in and I was waiting for the receptionist to tell Dave that the €52 he had paid on his hotel app was not the correct price. There were two doormen in the lobby and they were attending to each person and their luggage as they entered – well almost everyone, we were the exception. I could see Dave had been given a key and I knew then we had a real bargain for our last night.

We took the lift upstairs and the place was a little like being in *Star Trek*, very space age and new, green neon lights on the walls and silver doors to all the rooms. We dropped our bags and both collapsed on the beds knackered, and if I say so now, I was glad it was my last night. As a newly integrated member of the world's biking community, I had now made it to two and a half weeks, over 5,000km, and no major accidents. Tomorrow was a short dash home and I could then sleep in my own bed again. We snoozed for an hour and just chilled out, before a shower and a shave for our last night.

By 7pm we were ready for our last night on the town. As we exited the hotel we turned left. We had decided to look for a curry house for our last night, but we had only walked 300m before we decided to have a beer in the first bar we came to. There were a few locals sitting inside drinking, and we sat outside and ordered two small beers from the waitress when she came out. The beer turned up and we were on the Estrella draft once again. We sat having a bit of banter about the events of today – almost running out of fuel, chasing the storms away – as well as one or two of our wonderful moments on the journey to date.

What happened next was to be the most surreal and beautiful finish to the journey we could ever have imagined. The waitress came out and served each of us with a plate of burger and chips. Yes, a small burger and small portion of chips were placed on a plate before us. We insisted, or tried to insist, that we had not ordered the food, but she just looked back, smiled and told us that beer gave free tapas. This was unbelievable. We had a good chuckle at our luck and tucked into the small portion. At worst it meant that when we got to the curry house we would have to miss the starter and go straight for a main course.

We polished off the food and decided we had to have another beer as a thank you for such great tapas. So Dave ordered two more beers from the bar after spending a penny. We were once again enjoying the beer when the waitress came out and this time served us a really large portion of deep-fried parsnips with a caramel sauce drizzled over them.

This was unreal. It was a waste of time arguing, as we knew what the answer was – beer gives tapas.

By now we had resigned ourselves to the fact that we were not going to get a curry tonight – it was tapas and beer. So we tucked into the parsnips and polished them off too, as well as the beer. It was my turn to order this time and I popped inside and brought the beers back with me. I had a brief conversation with a couple sitting inside who were sharing a beer with the guy behind the bar and the waitress who had been serving us. It turned out that the waitress and the barman were married and owned the bar. I tried to buy them all a drink but they would not have it.

Sitting down again, Dave asked me what was coming this time. I had no idea, although I was just as eager to find out. We didn't have to wait too long before the waitress came out and delivered the next course, rough-cut potato chips with fried onions and a fried egg on top. This was heaven. We tucked in, and by now both Vanessa and Caroline were being bombarded with pictures and messages whilst we were drinking and eating. They too were just as inquisitive to know what was coming out each time we ordered beer.

Having been out now for only an hour, we had eaten almost our fill. We decided we still wanted a beer but were not sure that we needed more food. However, our stomachs were still talking, so we ordered beer again, but we were going to make this our last plate of food. The beers were really going down well tonight, and by the time the food appeared we needed a refill, but we insisted on no more food. Our waitress took the order but first she gave us a plate of fried sardines and mashed potato. Once again we took a couple of pictures and sent them to the girls, who were waiting to know what we got. Vanessa was laughing so much I could almost hear her and she was a hundred miles away. "You don't eat fish," she messaged.

"No," I replied, "but I got the mashed potato, Dave got the fish."

We were stuffed. It was just before 9pm, and we were wanting just the one more beer, but were both adamant no more food. This time when the barman came out we ordered beer but insisted no food, please no food. He smiled and nodded his head. Our last beer for the journey was delivered to our table, and we toasted each other. I thanked Dave for getting me so far and he thanked me for being a good companion. It was starting to feel real now, the journey was almost over.

We paid the bill, which came to €24 for six beers each and all the food we had eaten. We'd had a few real bargains on this journey but this one was right up at the top, and stood out as a great evening, with money very well spent, a full stomach and maybe one beer too many, as we wobbled back the 300m to   the   hotel.

Chapter 22

Breakfast for Kings as Lard Arse and Fat Man Make it Home

Tuesday, 2 October

26°C – blue skies and light clouds

169km to the journey's end

I was dressed and waiting to go for breakfast at 8am today. The hotel reservation came with breakfast, so it was a free meal before we left. Dave was feeling very delicate, and he had been up and down most of the night. My money was on the fish he had eaten the night before in the bar, as it was the only thing I had not eaten and I was fine. He was not having any of it though, but he was going to skip breakfast. Apparently, he hadn't dare fart all night, poor guy, just in case he left a mark in his jim-jams! I left him to it and headed down on my own.

I entered the restaurant where breakfast was being served and was asked to wait until seated by the front of house person, which was a first. I asked for a table for two just in case Dave did make it, even if it was just for a coffee. I got myself a coffee, placed it on my table and took a walk around the self-service buffet. This was a treat to finish the trip with. To start there was toast made from several different artisan breads, with jams and marmalade. There was also a choice of over twenty sliced hams, salamis and cheeses to go with it. Then you could choose from over ten different cereals or mueslis and any form of milk you wished, including tiny chocolate buttons and mini marshmallows to top it off with. Then it was on to the hot breakfast, where you could choose from made-to-order omelette, poached egg, fried egg or boiled egg. There was also bacon, pork sausage and chorizo sausage, mushrooms, fried tomatoes, hash browns and fried carrots – don't ask why, but someone must like them.

Moving on, if you still had room there were more than a dozen different mini pastries with white icing over them, chocolate sauce drizzled over others and a whole assortment of fillings too, not forgetting the chocolate cake and mini homemade fruit trifles with the fresh cream. This was a banquet fit for a king and the way I was feeling this morning, with the excitement of getting home soon, I was about to fill my boots.

Coffee and pastries to start with, I let my sweet tooth take over. Then another coffee and a plate of bacon and two fried eggs with two pieces of toast. I skipped the carrots and left them for Dave. I had to pause then, well, for all of about two minutes, whilst I waited for the area around the chocolate cake to become accessible, then I headed for a double helping with one final coffee. As I sat down to my cake, Dave walked in. "Jesus," he said, "I'm gutted." Yes, he was missing out on the best start to a day we had had all journey and it was free too. He had a black coffee and before too long we were checking out and fixing our cases for the last time before we headed home.

The N-340 carries on from Motril nearly all the way into Malaga, so our plan was to stay with it. Once we got to Malaga, we were hoping to miss the A-7 autovia and head back to Marbella via the towns of Coín and Ojén, then drop into Marbella a few miles from my lodge.

It was 9am when we left, intercoms working and all excited for the finish line. The first hour felt like we were back in the mountains, as we were climbing slightly then dropping down, but most exciting was that the road hugged the coast so tight we could almost feel the sea spray as we rode along this twisting and windy section. There was very little traffic and that helped with the enjoyment of the ride. We were finishing the journey with some fantastic roads that would give us both a very positive ending to this day.

Dave was leading, as he mostly did, and that suited me fine. We were chatting as we enjoyed the road and ride along the coast, feeling extremely lucky to have been able to carry out this journey and both thankful it had been accident free, despite my wobble on the second day that was now long forgotten. It wasn't too long before I heard for the last time, "It's twisty time, see you soon," and Dave was off, and I could not blame him. The road went into full-on twisty overload for about 6km and Dave was going to fill his boots one last time. I went for it too but it was the last day and it was in the back of my mind that I wanted to get back in one piece.

Dave had done a great job helping me around the whole peninsular and I didn't want to bugger it all up with a few hours to go. The kilometres travelled had just passed 5,200km, just under 3,300 miles, and this was my first two and half weeks of riding a motorcycle, so I was proud of myself too. I did enjoy the road this morning though, with its long wide corners, and we were dipping in and out of coastal coves and inlets, followed by a small straight section, before once again returning to the left- and right-hand twisties. Then it would start all over again and again, and this section felt like it was going on for ever. It was a great start to the last day.

It was closing in on 10.30am and we had been riding for almost an hour and a half, so it was coffee time. Dave was feeling a bit better, probably because of the fresh sea air and great roads. We pulled over to the left into a small car park, which belonged to a small shopping complex. When I say small, there were only twenty parking spaces and six shops, four of which were estate agents, one a small general store, and a nice little café right on the beachfront looking out south into the Mediterranean. Parking up we were both buzzing a little, as this was our last stop before the last section home and completion of the journey.

We sat and took some shade as Dave was still feeling a little dicky. We ordered coffee, and still Dave didn't want to eat. I didn't either, as I was still overflowing from my 'little' breakfast. We watched the sea for fifteen minutes, finished our coffees, then it was that time, the journey back to Marbella. We discussed the route back and agreed that Dave would stay in front until we were able to pick up the A-7 autovia, at which time I would shoot out in front and lead us around Malaga, trying to miss the worst of the traffic. Then I would take us as agreed via Coín and Ojén into the back of Marbella and home.

It was another 30km of great coastal roads, which really was a dream way to end the journey. We were chasing the twisties. Along one section, with Dave being about 200–300m ahead of me, I was doing all I could to stay with him. He was making it look all too easy to stay where he was. He was instructing me once again as to what was up and coming on the road ahead of me – sharp left, short straight into a long right-hand at speed, don't be afraid to use the speed.

As I was coming out of the long right-hander I got a message, "Deer to the right just crossing the road in front of me." Then, "Now heading up the cliff face." I tried to see the deer on my way past but it was Dave who was to be the only one of us to view the beast.

The A-7 was all too soon upon us, and we turned right just after La Cala del Moral and took the road west. It was now nearly noon and the traffic was building up, so I headed out in front. It even looked like we could get a rain shower. We stayed with the A-7 through a couple of large tunnels and a four-lane section of the autovia for just over 30km and finally took our last fuel stop as we turned right on to the A-357 north of Malaga. Staying with this main artery we then took the smaller A-7059 heading now for Coín, which was about a twenty-minute ride away.

Once again we were on some fine roads with great surfaces and little to no traffic. Just before we came to Coín we joined the main A-355 to Marbella that would lead us past Ojén and into the back of Marbella, over the mountains and down to sea level. It would be the last blast before we arrived home. The road was a large single lane with the occasional overtaking lane if needed.

I was still in front, as I knew this road very well, and I could push just that little harder now that I was in the comfort zone, knowing what was ahead on the road and where the corners were going to take me. It was a great finish too. I could see two cars ahead and a lorry a short distance in front of them, and I knew that there was an overtaking lane coming up ahead and that the road would bear left, giving me full view of the road in front of the truck and trailing cars. If I timed it right I could take all three vehicles and be back in front before any of them had had time to react.

I was in luck. I was right behind the left-hand corner of the first car, about ten metres back, as the road opened up and I could view the overtaking lane up to the left and the corner swooping away. One last check to make sure there was nothing on the other side coming at me or coming up behind me, then I opened the bike up and went from 65kph to 140kph in seconds. I was past the two cars before they had even seen the overtaking lane, or had chance to react. The lorry was just pulling right into the inside lane as I approached it and I was past him too. It was a perfect manoeuvre and I was pleased and brimming with confidence, but also now I had to tell myself to pull it back together as we had only 10km to go. Dave joined me a few seconds later. He had been caught by one of the cars and struggled to pass the lorry too.

We were now finishing the journey as we headed down past Ojén and into the industrial shopping area of Marbella at the La Canãda. We slowly made our way around the two roundabouts, then around the long right-hand swooping corner to enter on to the A-7 once again, but this time heading back towards Malaga and to the El Rosario area of the city. It was a right off the A-7 just past the main Marbella hospital and then back through the urbanisation and the wooded area, finally turning into the driveway of the lodge.

It was for me a very proud achievement. I had travelled over 5,300km on this bike and around the whole coastline of Spain and Portugal, not forgetting the Pyrenees. It had been my opening adventure of what I am hoping will be a great hobby in the coming years. I would not want to have shared the journey with anybody but my good friend Fat Man Dave. Without him I really don't think it would have been the same.

Chapter 23

The Morning After

Arriving back that afternoon just after 2pm, we both collapsed for an hour and just chilled out. It was great to see Vanessa, and Dave caught up with Caroline over the phone too. We mooched about that afternoon and eventually headed out in the evening for a pizza for dinner, just a short walk from the lodge. Thankfully Dave was feeling better than he had done in the morning and managed to get some food that evening, although he did stay off the beer.

Dave headed off by 8.30am on the Wednesday morning. I felt really guilty that he would need to ride another 1,000km just to get his ferry the following evening to sail back to the UK. We thanked each other for the last time and I wished him a safe journey back. He headed out and I mounted the bike for the last time too. It was back to Jac in the hire shop to return the bike. I explained that I had had one small incident whilst on the journey and he looked over the damage and told me there was no charge. For that I thanked him and also told him he would get a mention in my book for it. There you go Jac, you're in the book.

Dave messaged later that evening to let me and Vanessa know he was safe and at his hotel for the evening. I headed for bed very early that night, just after 8.30pm, and awoke after 8am the following day, the Thursday. Dave had messaged early in the morning to let me know he had already hit the final leg of the ride north, and another six hours later he messaged again to let me know he was at the port and checking in for the ferry.

He arrived safely home the following day, having travelled over 5,000 miles, with the additional mileage he had done to get to me in southern Spain and his return journey home. This had made his adventure a real mammoth journey, and for that, once again, I say thank you Dave.

So, looking back, did I enjoy the whole experience? Absolutely. Would I do it again? Most definitely. I fully enjoyed every part of the journey, from the fishing the year before to all the beers we drank throughout the whole journey of planning and riding. It was a fantastic dream come true for the two of us.

I'm just wondering what and where the next journey will be though. What I will say is that I'm sure it won't be at the time of Caroline and Fat Man's wedding anniversary in September. I get the feeling he won't be able to come out with me again during that month.

A Final Word from Fat Man Dave

It's true to say my first thoughts as Martin first discussed this trip were, here we go again, another mad idea from a recently retired man who was clearly having difficulty with all the spare time he had on his hands. Let's be honest, he is in his early fifties (looks a lot older), and has no experience of riding anything with two wheels. His previous plan had been for us to do a car rally across Africa in a beaten-up wreck that had to be over fifteen years old, but thankfully Vanessa brought that daft idea to a swift end due her concerns for his safety.

I have been good friends with Martin for many years and he has never shown the slightest interest in my great passion of riding motorbikes. He actually expressed a dislike, as he thought them to be dangerous, noisy and ridden too fast by men that needed to grow up. So, when he first discussed the idea of this trip I expected it to fizzle out, and he would soon move on to his next brilliant idea, but clearly not.

The original idea of doing the trip on hired 125cc step-through scooters did appeal initially, as it would be away from the norm for me. I have covered most of Europe numerous times over the years with very fast, experienced riders. We never really went there to enjoy the scenery, it was all about the thrill of hitting the twisties as fast as possible and whether we could hit the rev limiter in sixth gear down the autobahn. Nothing calm and peaceful about these trips, just full on, fast and adrenaline filled. This trip, if it came off, would be the exact opposite, which interested me.

Martin didn't give up on his new brilliant idea and I only realised he was really serious when he announced he was going to do his full motorbike test. Bit of a shock to me really, but then the plusses were going to be using my own bike (not having to hire a scooter), and enjoy the scenery, as I didn't want the pace to be outside of Martin's comfort zone.

Whether he was brave or naive at the time I wasn't sure, as passing the full direct access motorcycle test is not easy these days. But again he surprised me by passing the practical test first time. A great accomplishment. So the adventure was on.

I left home, rode down to Portsmouth, took a ferry to Santander, then a two-day journey through central Spain, skirting Madrid, and arrived safely at Martin's place near Malaga. On the day I arrived we headed out on the bikes for a test run, before leaving for our adventure the next morning.

How confident and capable would he be riding the bike with luggage, considering it had been months since last riding on the day of his test? The outcome of this little shakedown run for me at the time was extremely important, as his ability to handle the bike was going to dictate the whole of the journey and I had to ensure I planned the daily route length and difficulty in line with Martin's abilities. I hate having to use the word 'impressed' when it involves Martin, as we have a friendship that has thrived for years on abuse, sarcasm and negativity towards each other, but credit where credit's due, he rode with confidence and showed great bike skills around some extremely tight, twisty, hilly roads.

So, the next morning we set off on our adventure, which Martin has described very accurately within this book.

For me the positives on this trip were many:

1) Seeing Martin's terrified, shocked face as he took off his helmet after a narrow escape with the Armco barrier. He survived without injury and learned a very valuable lesson, which I believe helped him remain safe for the rest of the trip and built up his capabilities before becoming too confident.

2) Spending time doing something I love with an old friend, only two of us, not a large group, with all the complex dynamics that can bring.

3) The pleasure of seeing Martin progress from a novice to a competent rider.

4) That first beer in the evening after a long hot ride and, of course, the free tapas that normally accompanied it.

5) The sheer beauty of Spain. The contrasts of dry and arid to green and lush, flat plains to high mountains, we saw it all and I have many memories of places I wish to return to. There is so much more to Spain, away from the tourist spots you see on television. It's a truly amazing and beautiful country.

And the negatives:

1) The sheer pain and discomfort of having to pack up that bloody tent with the worst hangover I've ever had in my life. Never again!!!

2) Sleeping in the same room as Martin every night. I will spare you the details.

3) Being away from my wife for nearly a month. I did miss my other best mate.

4) Blooming satnav. I would never be without it and consider it an essential; however, when it plays up it can be incredibly frustrating.

So, the last comments in my little section of this book are to thank my very lovely wife for happily letting me go, considering this was the second year running I was away on her birthday (with Martin) and on our wedding anniversary (I'm a very, very, lucky man), and of course to my old mate Martin for this great adventure.

Dave

I might be a Fat Man but never a Lard Arse!

Summary of the Journey

If you made it this far then thank you for taking the time to read my journey with Dave. I hope you enjoyed it as much as we did, firstly riding the Iberian Peninsula and secondly writing this book.

If Fat Man Dave is still speaking to me, I would like to thank him for his support over the whole trip. I know that without him I would never have been able to get through the whole journey. I'm sure this won't be the last of our adventures and I genuinely look forward to the next time we dream up another adventure, provided it's not at the time of Dave's wedding anniversary.

It's important for me that if you the reader think there are good points or bad points about the book, even comments you would like to make on the book, however large or small, for my potential readers, that you please leave a review. Please tell people just what you thought about the book. For small publishers such as me it's a huge statement to receive reviews and naturally helps potential readers understand exactly what they can expect form this book.

If you have any further questions or comments that you would like to ask me personally, please feel free to contact me, Martin Barber at the following email address:

martindbarber66@gmail.com

I am only too pleased to answer your questions.

Martin D Barber.

aka Señor Lard Arse ☺

I mentioned my editor, Ivan, in the acknowledgements earlier, but as an additional thank you, I've invited him to include his business details here, just in case you read this book, are inspired to write your own, and need a good editor.

Coachhouse Business Services
Copy-editing & Proofreading Professional
Ivan Butler MBA
Email: ivanbutler897@btinternet.com
www.coachhousebusinessservices.co.uk